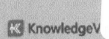 KnowledgeV

REMEDY ®

The Formula for an Evolving Human Performance Culture

D. Bowman, T. Brumfield, K. Hallaran,
J. Merlo, D. Sowers

i

Remedy: The Formula for an Evolving Human Performance Culture

Copyright © 2022 -2024 David Bowman, Todd Brumfield, Kenneth Hallaran, James Merlo, Dave Sowers

ISBN: 979-8-9856099-3-6 (Print)

ISBN: 979-8-9856099-4-3 (eBook)

Disclaimer

For information regarding permission, write to:

The Zebra Ink

publisher@thezebraink.com

The Zebra Ink, PO BOX 16664, Rocky River, OH 44116

www.thezebraink.com

Printed in the United States of America

Cover Design: Monica Hughes

Interior Design: Voices in Print

10 9 8 7 6 5 4 3 2

CONTENTS

In Praise of KnowledgeVine's
REMEDY

"We implemented the REMEDY Human Performance training several years ago, and we've been incredibly pleased with the results. The organizational alignment it brings from speaking the same language in HP has had positive effects outside of safety performance. The in-field coaching has been instrumental in helping us establish an effective organizational culture—we haven't had a lost-time injury since implementing Human Performance with KnowledgeVine."

~ Bryan Beadle, Vice President of Transmission
Utility Lines Construction Services

"Our organization adopted KnowledgeVine's Human Performance program and it transformed our thinking about safety and the way we work. It was much more than just a safety program...it was a new approach for running our business. We are a better company as a result."

~ Robbie Laborde, CLECO
Chief Operations and Sustainability Officer

"Our Total Recordable Incident Rate was too high, so we called KnowledgeVine to implement REMEDY Human Performance training and in-field coaching. A year later our TRIR was down 40% and the utility we work with was complementary to our performance improvements. Since then, we have expanded the REMEDY training into other regions so we can duplicate these results across the company."

~ David Baker, Vice President Power and Gas,
MP Technologies LLC

"For years we had not gone a month without an OSHA recordable accident. After implementing the KnowledgeVine process, we went almost six months between OSHA recordable events. Additionally, we were able to improve our Recordable Incident Rate (from 2.05 to 1.68), our Lost Workday Incident Rate (from 1.23 to 0.50), and our insurance claims (from 128 to 65). Once workers realized that Chain Electric and KnowledgeVine were invested in their safety and were committed to improving the entire organization, HR reported the turnover rate was reduced by 40%."

~ Tim Adam, former Director of Safety and Training
Chain Electric

FOREWORD

Collectively, our team has spent the better part of our lives—definitely the last 30 years—working to protect the plant, the vehicle, the company, and most importantly the human capital we have had the pleasure to work beside. We have seen the concept of HUMAN PERFORMANCE (HP) work and we have seen it fail. We have conducted countless root cause analyses, accident investigations, and most importantly, after-action reviews (AARs), where we have been able to praise and coach the effective use of hazard identification (HP Traps) and successful remediation of RISKS (HP Tools) resulting in error-free performance.

We have learned a great deal on our journeys, and we are excited to share what we have learned. The successful application of HP is worth the effort. It's not a pill, a program, or a one-day class—it's a cultural-driven change, which pays dividends in more ways than can be imagined. We will explore the lesson we probably already knew but are reminded of daily; *the organization's leadership is the critical component.* Effective leaders know their culture and thrive in its strength. They also continuously monitor and strive to strengthen its weaknesses, especially in those cases where the errors in the workplace have potentially extreme consequences.

The collections of ideas, theories, and applications in this book bring together the work of leaders and prominent scholars from around the world who are applying the data, science, and application of the psychological, social, and organizational factors that influence behavior in the work and home environments.

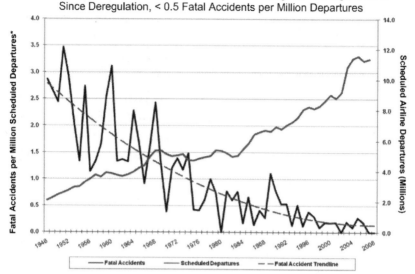

With Each Decade, U.S. Airline Safety Has Improved
Since Deregulation, < 0.5 Fatal Accidents per Million Departures

* Scheduled passenger and cargo operations of U.S. air carriers operating under 14 CFR 121; NTSB accident rates exclude incidents resulting from illegal acts

Source: National Transportation Safety Board (NTSB)

Aviation Graphic[1]

One of the best examples of how the use of Human Performance changed an industry is in commercial aviation. The graphic above presents the number of commercial airline takeoffs in contrast to the number of fatalities. For the first few decades, technological advancements were the key instrument that drove down the risks and made flight safer. However, as illustrated in this figure, the late 80s showed an increase in fatal accidents (shown by the spike or rise of fatalities), largely due to the poor implementation of technology and automation into the flight systems and the resultant loss of situation awareness and crew coordination. The aviation community as a whole began to focus on near misses, instituted a still wildly successful near-miss database, and increased the focus on Human Performance and Crew Resource Management. The success is evident as the industry hit the zero target with no US carrier fatalities for over a decade, making air travel one of the safest methods of travel available and building a safety culture that is second to none. Technology could only get us so far, as the human capital became the critical asset for truly reliable, safe flight.

Creating a culture is not an easy task. The pages of this book, *REMEDY: The Formula for an Evolving Human Performance Culture,* are filled with an enormous amount of useful information. *REMEDY* is organized to first achieve an understanding of the broad strategy before it presents day-to-day tactics and techniques to help shape the ORGANIZATIONAL CULTURE.

If you know you need a Human Performance culture in your organization, you're in the right place.

If you're not sure where to start, you're in the right place. If you previously tried to implement Human Performance and the culture never evolved, you're in the right place.

If you're currently working to create a Human Performance culture and feel like you have plateaued, you're in the right place.

REMEDY will present the broad strategy and specific tactics needed to create and sustain a Human Performance culture to help reduce the frequency and severity of human error in your workplace.

REMEDY offers easily understandable guidance for executives and leaders to prepare themselves and their organizations for the challenges of cultural change, which are critical for the successful implementation of Human Performance. This book has been written for the incredibly talented men and women, our human capital, who put themselves in harm's way every day to perform the critical tasks and work that keep our nation strong. We strongly believe this definitive book will contribute to enhancing the effectiveness, safety, and well-being of our human capital—the most important asset of any organization.

Dr. James Merlo
Vice President of Operational Excellence
KnowledgeVine

REMEDY®

"When you first learned HUMAN PERFORMANCE, was it easy or difficult?"

This was a question posed to KnowledgeVine by one of their very first clients. The room was filled with foremen, general foremen, safety professionals, and executive leadership of a utility group. KnowledgeVine had been hired to come in to help the organization adopt Human Performance practices. This was in the early days when KnowledgeVine consisted of Co-Owners David Bowman, Dave Sowers, and a couple of other team members. Dave Sowers was facilitating this client training and telling the class how simple it was to look for HP traps and to mitigate them with HP tools. He sensed there was some hesitation in the room and his suspicions were confirmed when one of the foremen raised his hand and asked the question above.

He paused momentarily to think about this question and his response. Apparently, there was too much of a delay as the foreman interjected, "See. It IS difficult!" Dave quickly replied, "No, I remember it being easy. I'm just trying to figure out why we're struggling in this room right now."

As he stood there thinking about his experience as a young nuclear power operator trying to learn about this new thing called *Human Performance* (HP) it occurred to him what the problem might be. He shared, "I was first introduced to HP as part of my initial training at the nuke plant. The HP course made perfect sense but now that I'm thinking about it, I didn't really learn how to apply HP to my job until I was in the plant. If I had a question, I could simply turn to the person next to me, who'd been using HP for years, and they could coach me through it. Using HP methods was a requirement, not an option. It was part of the culture and something they did every day; I only had to follow along. I didn't have the option of waiting it out to see if this brand-new HP thing was going away. HP was part of the culture long before I arrived and would be there long after I was gone. I think it was easy for me because I stepped into an HP culture and needed to fall in line. I think it's difficult today because I'm not asking you to adapt to an existing culture, I'm asking you to CREATE a new culture—and that's a different challenge altogether."

KnowledgeVine began with the goal to help organizations leverage Human Performance benefits in the same way as the nuclear power and aviation industries do. We quickly realized this was a bigger challenge than anticipated. You can't simply *do what nuclear and aviation do* because you don't have their cultures. Your hierarchy, structure, goals, experiences, priorities, and influences are different, so any attempt to *cut and paste* their HP processes into your organization is going to be difficult. There's also the dynamic of motivation. Nuclear and aviation have regulators that require Human Performance processes. Your incentives are different when you *have to* versus when you *want to*. It doesn't take long to realize that the formula used within other cultures won't work for yours.

> *Simply put, adopting Human Performance is difficult because your culture is resisting it every step of the way.*

This doesn't mean you can't implement Human Performance. It just means you must figure out ways to work within the culture you already have to gain small improvements and gradually turn the culture over time. Culture resists change, but it's not immovable. There are many organizations that are able to turn their culture to great success; but they don't do it overnight. There are many more organizations that tried and failed. If you've witnessed your own organization, try new program after new program but nothing seemed to stick, then you recognize how strongly culture resists change.

If you think creating a Human Performance culture can be done quickly, then this isn't the book for you. We know that culture change is NOT a one-size-fits-all approach; that's why this book isn't called *Six Easy*

Steps to Change Your Culture or *Culture Change in Five Minutes a Day.* If you've tried to implement HP and failed or wanted to try but didn't know where to start because you sense your organization *isn't ready,* you'll find your answers in the following pages.

So, let's answer the question, "Why is creating a new culture so difficult?" Simply put, you often don't have a plan to manage the change you want to see. You likely just threw out a new program and hoped it would stick. You must also consider HOW you are going to create change; not just WHAT you hope to change.

KnowledgeVine started taking a hard look at all the prevailing literature, guiding documents, and STANDARDS for Human Performance and noticed a commonality; they all gave a vision of what a fully functional HP process looks like but didn't tell you *how to get there from scratch.* In most cases, this was acceptable because they were speaking to organizations that were further down the road and had existing cultures to create and sustain improvement. But for everyone new to the game, it's a recipe for failure to emulate nuclear and aviation. You can't see them already standing on third base and say, "Just start there."

One case in point is the Department of Energy's *Human Performance Improvement Handbook,* which has a formula for the strategic approach to Human Performance RE + MC → 0E. By way of brief explanation:

RE is to *reduce errors* or those in-the-moment actions taken by the individual.

MC is to *manage controls* or those organizational influences that either set workers up for success or create challenges, which they must navigate.

Addressing both of these will yield zero events or 0E. It's a great formula keeping you focused on the idea that error reduction is the responsibility of the organization AND the individual contributor. As mentioned earlier, if you're already on the right road, then RE + MC → 0E is a good roadmap. If you're not already on this road, then there needs to be a plan to manage this organizational change and help you find the right path for your culture.

If you've read this far, you likely understand that a Human Performance culture is what's best for your organization. At KnowledgeVine we have seen the positive effects an HP culture creates and are driven to help you build and sustain one. When the entire organization is engaged and everyone understands how to make it work, growth and improvement climb steadily. Anywhere there are humans there is the potential for human error, and Human Performance can greatly reduce human error. This is true for any organization. It doesn't matter whether your work involves making micro-chips or potato chips, it can be done more safely, more efficiently, and with fewer mistakes.

There are many ways to go about error reduction, but we are going to share what our 150-plus combined years of experience have taught us about sustainable and successful utilization of Human Performance. This experience, across numerous organizations, allows KnowledgeVine to share what works best and where the pitfalls may lie. While these tactics are universal, you may find there is a need for some customization to work best within your unique culture. Take what is offered here and make it yours. Tweak what needs to be tweaked to make it fit.

In the following pages, you'll find a lot of excellent information about adopting a Human Performance culture but if you don't get started, you'll never get there. Of course, you don't want to just take off in some random direction. You need to understand a few important things about this journey, or it will be the latest in a long line of false starts.

- Why do bad things keep happening? (Human Error)
- Where can you turn to stop Human Error? (Human Performance)
- Where are you now? (Understand the current culture)
- What is the path forward? (What does "good" look like)

- How do you keep the momentum going? (Prevent DRIFT and keep improving)

- What does each person need to do to accomplish the above?

All of these considerations must be looked at through the lens of culture change and how to understand, influence, and sustain an evolving culture from every level of the organization.

Creating a culture is not an easy task and there are many moving parts involved. The pages of this book are filled with an enormous amount of useful information, but this comes with some risk; you may fail to see the forest for the trees. Because of this, *REMEDY* is organized to first gain an understanding of the broad strategy (the forest), before it presents day-to-day tactics to help shape the culture (the trees). While there are many chapters supporting the strategy and tactics of Human Performance culture change, this book is broadly organized as follows:

PART I: THE FOREST—BIG IDEAS

- Know what you're up against by understanding the strength and importance of organizational culture.

- Look at how individuals are simultaneously creating the culture while also being influenced by it (The CULTURE CYCLE).

- Learn the broad strategy for creating a Human Performance culture (**REMEDY** FORMULA).

- Understand how each level of the organization can start working together toward the common goal of creating a Human Performance culture (**REMEDY** MATRIX).

- Determine WHY you get certain BEHAVIORS to target your corrective actions (WHY).

- Develop a change management strategy with Human Performance in mind (DIAS).

PART II: THE TREES—SPECIFIC ACTIONS

- Learn more about the actions each individual can take every day.
- Dive deeper into the REMEDY Matrix to help everyone understand the tactics they can use to create and sustain a Human Performance culture.

To keep all of the useful information organized in your head as you progress through *REMEDY*, remember: Part I is the overall strategy and concepts necessary to understand in order to implement some of the specific tactics found in Part II. A good analogy is learning to drive. In Part I, you get a learner's permit to understand the rules of the road and begin to understand the basics of vehicle operation. In Part II, you learn specific driving tactics (and practice them daily) until these behaviors are well ingrained and you are adept at avoiding disaster. Buckle up!

The HIGHLIGHTED words noted throughout the book are found in a glossary in the back of the book for greater understanding of each term.

REMEDY$^\beta$

The Formula for an Evolving Human Performance Culture

PART I
THE FOREST
BIG IDEAS

REMEDY®

CHAPTER 1

CULTURE WILL FIGHT YOUR NEW PROGRAMS

For individuals, character is destiny; for organizations, culture is destiny.

~ Tony Hsieh (1973 – 2020)

On January 28, 1986, the Space Shuttle Challenger was 73 seconds into its flight when an explosion occurred resulting in the breakup of the orbiter and the death of all seven crew members aboard. Subsequent investigations found there was a failure of two redundant O-rings on the right solid rocket booster which allowed pressurized gas to burn through the wall of an adjacent, external fuel tank. The resultant explosion caused a separation of the rockets and orbiter. The orbiter, which included the crew compartment, was broken apart by aerodynamic forces and disintegrated off the coast of Cape Canaveral, Florida. [2]

Ronald Reagan created the Rogers Commission to investigate the tragedy. In its final report, the Rogers Commission was highly critical of NASA's culture and decision-making processes. At the time, NASA's culture allowed productivity pressure to overcome safety concerns. Sound familiar? The rocket booster contractor, Thiokol, knew the low temperatures at the launch pad that day would compromise the O-rings and recommended a *no-go* on the flight. NASA, however, asked them to reconsider their no-go recommendation. The launch had already been delayed three times and was also closely watched by the public as the mission crew included schoolteacher, Christa McAuliffe. Thiokol engineers reversed their position and declared the solid rocket motors ready for launch.

The Challenger disaster resulted in a 32-month hiatus in the Space Shuttle program as NASA worked to redesign some shuttle components, establish better processes to address safety concerns, bolster crew safety systems, and improve their organizational culture.

Think about how motivated NASA was to repair their culture. The eyes of the world witnessed the tragic results of a culture that was subject to productivity pressure, stove piped information flow, and an undesirable yield in performance. This example illustrates the importance of culture at all levels of the organization: the executives, the leaders, and the workers. They were compelled by the highest levels of government to improve their culture. NASA's very existence depended on getting it right as many politicians openly considered whether NASA was too broken and should be scrapped altogether.

NASA worked tirelessly to regain public trust and to fix their broken culture. After almost three years, NASA successfully launched the Space Shuttle Endeavor. Problem solved and NASA is back on track, right?

Sadly, no.

On February 1, 2003, the Space Shuttle Columbia disintegrated as it reentered the atmosphere, killing all seven crew members. An independent review by the Columbia Accident Investigation Board once again cited NASA's still broken safety culture as a contributing factor to the tragedy.[3]

It took NASA years of trying to shift their culture and they still didn't get it right, despite a massive amount of governmental oversight. However, you often think a new process or program can transform your organizational culture in a matter of months. Organizational Culture is strong and often resists change and the best of intentions. Understanding the culture and how it works is key to any change process, especially when you want to implement a system that addresses worker behaviors, like Human Performance. Culture can be a tough thing to define but understanding it remains the key to shaping it.

In the words of Phil McAlister, NASA's director of commercial spaceflight development, "All organizations have a culture, and it's almost like the DNA associated with an organization. It has a history and a memory. Even though people come and go, that DNA is always there."

What is your organization's culture? It's not defined by your mission, vision, and values statements. These are simply statements of what your organization aspires to be. Your true culture lies much deeper in the organization.

> *It's the sum of the behaviors of every individual that defines your organization's culture.*

To change the culture, you must change the individual behaviors. But you often don't look at behaviors; you look at results. You often look at good outcomes and assume they were the product of good behaviors. For example, you send a worker out to complete a job, and hours later they return to report the task is completed on schedule with no accidents or injuries. Good job, right? Nope. Good result! The worker could have violated every safety rule in the book, exhibiting the worst behaviors, but with a little bit of luck still got the right result. Or perhaps there were mistakes made but they weren't reported. From the manager's viewpoint, it was a job well done, when really it was poorly completed but fortunately successful. As you can see, good results aren't necessarily the product of good behaviors. Two vastly different cultures can arrive at the same result. The difference is the culture that exhibits safe behaviors can get there more consistently since they don't need to rely on the element of luck.

Now the question becomes, WHAT influences worker behaviors? The answer is—past experiences shape current beliefs. In the previous example, the worker believed they could take shortcuts or violate safety rules because they either did it exactly that way before and got away with it or can draw from similar experiences to believe there's a good chance that taking the risk will work out this time too.

Take glove use requirements as an example. Typically, a memo will be sent out stating a glove use requirement when particular work is performed. Cut and dried. Pretty simple. No wiggle room. However, for reasons like TIME PRESSURE, DISTRACTIONS, OVERCONFIDENCE, OR VAGUE GUIDANCE, workers may draw from their experiences and believe they can safely do this work without their gloves this time. Keep in mind, that this is most likely not your worst worker. It's probably closer to your average worker. Most have barehanded something they should have used gloves to handle, and now look at certain jobs with the belief that gloves would be nice but might not be necessary every time, despite the rule. Your belief that you can safely NOT use gloves will shape your behavior to not use gloves this time. Guess what? It worked out. No one was hurt so your experience is that you don't have to use gloves next time and again, not get hurt. Your past experiences shape your current beliefs, which influence your behaviors. The results of your behaviors become your latest experiences. Sound like a cycle? It is.

The image below represents the Culture Cycle—understanding it is essential to shaping your organization's culture.

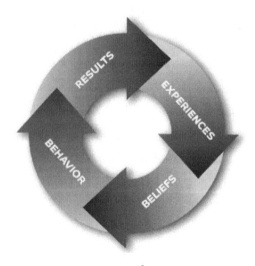

This is an overly simplified explanation upon which we will broadly expand about how your experiences shape your beliefs, which influence your behaviors, and that in turn drives good results. However, risky behaviors, with a little bit of luck, can also get good results. A good result creates a good experience which keeps the cycle going. A bad result creates a negative experience. This changes your beliefs which changes your behaviors to avoid that bad result. The cycle is shifting. A bad result isn't the only way the cycle can shift.

> *You can guide workers to better behaviors to get the good results and celebrate efforts to create a positive experience...influencing beliefs with the carrot instead of the stick.*

This might sound a little too much like psychobabble to have any relevance to your *nuts-and-bolts* world but it is important to have an understanding of what informs and motivates a person's behaviors. To make understanding the Culture Cycle easier, let's look at an example of how it applies to a common activity—driving.

When you drive there are rules stating how fast you can go for the given conditions. However, absent a physical limiter, you always have the option to speed. The reason you may choose to speed is that your previous experience with speeding worked out just fine; no tickets, no wrecks, and you arrived a little quicker. You had a neutral, or even positive, experience with speeding so your belief is that you can safely speed again. Or perhaps you have the quite common belief that the speed limit has some wiggle room. As long as you stay less than 10 miles over the speed limit most law enforcement officials won't stop you. Maybe you are moving with the flow of traffic and want to conform to the perceived social norm. Maybe you speed a little or maybe you speed a lot, but either way, your prior experience with speeding has shaped your current beliefs about speeding. Now the *behavior of speeding* is always an option.

If the experience is changed, you should start to see different behaviors. If every time your car crept one mile per hour over the speed limit you got a ticket or a fine mailed to you, you would have a different experience and you would be less inclined to speed. Follow the culture cycle. The result of the behavior of speeding is a ticket, and you don't like the experience of getting a ticket. Your belief now is that you shouldn't speed, so you can avoid the ticket experience. You change your behavior to obey the speed limit. The result is NOT speeding, and your experience is NOT getting a ticket or fine. Again, this is the stick approach; shaping behaviors to avoid negative experiences. However, you don't always need to experience negative outcomes to shape behaviors. You can often coach people to avoid negative results.

For example, if you were to visit the state of Washington, and the person at the rental car counter upon learning you are new to the area may coach you by saying, "Heads up. I don't know how it is where you're from, but there's no 10-mile-an-hour speeding buffer around here. They'll ticket you for any speed above the posted limit. It's best to set your cruise control a few miles under." This coaching will influence your beliefs and your behavior would be to carefully stay under the limit for the entirety of your trip, resulting in one less out-of-state driver speeding on the Washington roads. That's the culture of Washington drivers and you need to yield to it. This coaching can be likened to the often heard, "I don't know how they did it at your last job, but we don't do that here," coaching a new person will get about the organization's current culture. You don't need to experience the negative result; you just need coaching to avoid the negative experience.

Although you may not have a negative experience, your behaviors are shaped by the threat of the negative experience; but change doesn't always have to rely on avoiding negative experiences. Think about the different safe driving monitors various insurance companies offer. Some sort of device that plugs into your car's data link connector and monitors your driving behaviors like speeding, rapid accelerations, abrupt braking, or harsh cornering. After a few weeks of the device collecting data on your driving, your insurance rates can be lowered if your scores are good. These companies make it noticeably clear that if your driving scores are bad your rates will not go up. You have nothing to lose so there's no *stick*. However, they dangle the carrot of lower rates to help shape your behavior. They use other positive methods like vanishing deductibles or lowering rates after several years of no insurance claims; both of which are rewards to help shape good behaviors versus punishments for bad ones. This idea is well established in psychology literature and is important to be noted here. Punishment stops the undesired behavior, but positive reinforcement is needed to shape, acquire, and sustain desirable behavior.

Remember, your culture isn't your mission, vision, and values statements. It's the behaviors of each member of your team that defines your culture. This is why we look at how to influence individual beliefs, behaviors, results, and experiences to shape the actions of each person. If enough of the individuals in an organization are exhibiting new behaviors, then the culture of the organization is shifting towards this new norm. The group culture shifting toward this new behavior will have a feedback influence on individual behaviors. Individuals will quickly recognize this organizational norm and, in an effort to not stick out, will follow this norm themselves. As more people demonstrate *we don't do that here*, more people will not do that here. And round and round it goes until something else influences their beliefs in another direction. Just like the driving example, if no one else around you is exceeding the speed limit, you will tend to stay below the speed limit too.

It should start to be clear there are many ways to influence the Culture Cycle to create the kind of feedback loops that steer your culture in the right direction. In the subsequent chapters, we will address the ways you can influence the Culture Cycle to create a Human Performance culture. As you can imagine, there are no limits to the ways you can exert influence within your organization. To bring some structure to the conversation, we will look at the strategies for change management and the roadmap for each individual's role in supporting this strategy.

CHAPTER 2

REMEDY FORMULA
TO THE RESCUE

"If you fail to plan, you are planning to fail"
~ Benjamin Franklin (1706 - 1790)

In 2003, the Spanish Navy commissioned the construction of a new class of submarine, the S-80. The first submarine in this new class of electric-diesel boats was to be named the Isaac Peral, after the naval engineer who, in 1888, designed the first electric-powered sub for Spain. Although the design was in place, actual construction didn't start until 2007, due to economic concerns in Spain.

By 2013, with construction well underway, it was discovered that an engineer with the original design firm had misplaced a single decimal point which resulted in the miscalculation of the Isaac Peral's weight by one hundred tons. This additional weight meant the brand new, $600 million boat would be unable to resurface once submerged.

This might sound like a cautionary tale of the value of Human Performance tools, like Self-Checking or Peer-Checking, to prevent a simple human error in costing millions of dollars and years of lost time; and it is. However, what happened next tells a different story about the impact of a lack of planning.

Spain spent an additional $9 million dollars over 3 years to have the boat assessed and redesigned. It was decided that if the boat were lengthened by 33 feet, it would increase the buoyancy of the Isaac Peral enough to account for the additional weight of the submarine. Spain moved forward with the Peral's revised construction plan, and the S-80 now became the S-80 Plus. After five years of additional construction, with the project nearing completion, someone finally asked the question,

"When the Isaac Peral leaves the construction yard, where will it be parked, and will it fit?"

The answers to these questions were, "It's going to be parked in Cartagena and no, it won't fit."

The final cost of the boat had ballooned to $1.14 billion, almost double the original projected cost. Now the Spanish Navy needed to spend an additional $16 million dollars to dredge, widen, and lengthen the Cartagena docks so the S-80 Plus would have a place to park.

There was a plan. The design error caused a change to the plan. They failed to effectively manage this change and realize how it would impact the rest of the organization. Similarly, rolling out a new Human Performance process is a change to your current plan. How are you going to manage this change, so you also don't lose time, money, and effort on a process only to find yourself left with something you didn't quite have in mind and is possibly unworkable?

This is a great example of seeing the trees but missing the forest. While their attention was so focused on correcting the problem before them, they failed to consider the bigger picture. Change needed to happen but because of siloed thinking it was mismanaged and created further strife and angst.

Considering how you will manage change
is almost as important as what you're
going to change.

As discussed in the introduction, the DOE's Human Performance Improvement Handbook has a formula for the strategic approach to Human Performance: RE + MC → OE. While this is a great reminder that individuals AND the organization bear responsibility for SUSTAINING a Human Performance culture, it's not as relevant to groups looking to CREATE a Human Performance culture.

From the beginning, KnowledgeVine endeavored to make Human Performance easy to understand and apply for those who didn't have the benefit of an established HP culture. To accomplish this, we knew we needed to use more common language and include techniques for managing, identifying and controlling risk. Looking at the DOE formula, it's tough to say "Reduce Errors" if you really don't understand the risks that encourage errors. It's also difficult to say "Manage Controls" if you don't have a solid understanding of the risks you are trying to control. For this reason, we evolved the DOE formula of RE + MC → OE to provide a *north star* for organizations looking to CREATE a Human Performance culture: RE+M+ED=Y or REMEDY.

The REMEDY formula is broken down as follows:

RE—Reduce Errors. Eliminating those active, in-the-moment, individual errors. Things like selecting the wrong switch, operating the wrong breaker, closing the wrong valve, administering the wrong medication, or capturing the wrong information. Usually, the triggering action of an event or accident, but not the only cause.

M—Manage Risk. Identifying risk may be an individual effort, but effectively managing this risk requires a team approach. Everyone must do their part to mitigate risks whether that is observing the work in the field, providing proper guidance through coaching, or identifying the risk and making a conservative decision about the next step. You should strive to mitigate risks in all areas, whether it is a change in the existing processes, a deviation in the work plan, or a questionable piece of equipment that might lead to unwanted circumstances.

ED—Error Defenses. Understanding that the organization and work structures have an enormous influence on the worker's behaviors. Are we setting workers up for success by defending against errors or asking them to overcome error-likely situations?

Y—Yield. When individuals can reduce active errors, manage and mitigate risks, and strengthen error defenses to give the best chance of success, it will create an organization that is resilient against human error.

Later chapters will go into more specifics (the trees), but it's important to have a general understanding of the REMEDY formula as it relates to influencing the Culture Cycle.

Looking at the Culture Cycle again, you can begin to see how a strategy utilizing the REMEDY formula can influence your team's behaviors and results. Let's walk through a typical roll out of an organization's new HP process.

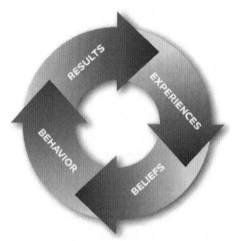

The first thing you need to do is to teach and inspire your people at all levels of the organization. After all, you can't expect employees to use HP if they don't know what that means. Sharing this information can be done in a variety of settings, from clicking through a PowerPoint, to sitting in a class in a conference room at the local Holiday Inn®. Whatever the medium, this learning is an attempt to influence the Culture Cycle by shaping the beliefs of the employee. The hope is that the training is effective, and the workers can see the personal benefits for themselves and will decide to give it a try the next time they are engaged in work.

Let's say their beliefs were indeed influenced by this training and they decided to look for HP Traps (the things that could encourage errors) and mitigate them with HP Tools (the techniques to prevent error); this is a new behavior. This new behavior should result in the safe, efficient, and accurate completion of work. The successful result should create a positive experience and the worker now has the belief that HP is personally beneficial, based on the training and their personal experience. In a perfect world, their belief in HP will influence subsequent behaviors and results, and positive experiences will ensue, reinforcing the cycle over and over. Human Performance now becomes the norm in your organization.

Not quite.

Of course, this isn't the way it actually works and there are several reasons why. Perhaps the training wasn't relevant, or otherwise lacking, and the worker never really gained the belief that HP was personally beneficial. Without any in-field coaching, the worker is left to stumble through their own interpretation of what *good looks like* as they try to apply classroom training to their in-field work. This experience is filled with frustration and uncertainty; the opposite of the positive experience you want. Often a lack of clear expectations from leadership makes HP behaviors seem optional, so there's no sense of obligation to do anything more than *be aware*. Probably most often, the culprit is a failure to see any appreciable difference in the result. If a worker can get the same result with the old, familiar behaviors, then why put the effort into this new, unfamiliar HP practice?

Most of the time your workers are remarkably successful at what they do. The problem is that the rare times it does go wrong, it can be fatal or result in significant injuries. There is no margin for error. You're asking your people to change the way they do something that most of the time delivers desirable results, and the experience has been good. You don't have the option of applying HP to jobs that never go right, because most jobs always go right. There's no motivation to fix the job because it doesn't feel broken. Even on the heels of a significant event (serious injury, fatality, major resource loss), most will rationalize that it's not a personal problem since, "I wouldn't have done XYZ, so that would never happen to me and my team."

For a short time, you might have been able to influence the engaged workers' beliefs and possibly get a temporary change in behavior. For the disengaged workers, you may have only gotten lip service as they play the odds that this latest program will fail, and they wait for this HP thing to go away. Either way, you are likely right back where you started. You didn't really change beliefs in any sustainable way. Workers didn't receive any in-field guidance or coaching and had to muddle their way through, so the overall experience was not positive. The behaviors were optional, therefore they opted to not engage in HP. There is no discernable difference in the results, so let's just go back to the way we used to do things. Culture wins again.

It should be clear that one-and-done training is not a sustainable solution and certainly has a low probability of shifting the culture. Even the addition of field guides or posters and signs does little to make this process any more successful. Soon the field guides are buried in a drawer, glove compartment, or toolbox, and posters and signs quickly become *background noise* to which no one gives any attention. You don't need to have the experience of a failed HP rollout to recognize these traps when trying to create change within an organization.

This reveals a significant pitfall; HOW you enact change is often just as important as WHAT you are changing.

The HOW needs to be more comprehensive than one-and-done training. Culture change also isn't a one-dimensional process. Unless you're living in a commune, different levels of the organization always have different roles and responsibilities. While both are important to the success of the organization, work in the boardroom is different from work in the toolroom. The failure to recognize distinctive roles within the organization has been one of the failures of many well-intentioned Human Performance initiatives.

One-size-fits-all does NOT fit Human Performance culture change.

CHAPTER 3

REMEDY MATRIX
BECAUSE ONE SIZE
DOES NOT FIT ALL

"Everyone has the will to win but very few have the will to prepare to win."

~ Vince Lombardi (1913 – 1970)

For an organization to be successful in any endeavor, it would be wise to prepare each member of their team for their specific role in the shared goal. Everyone doesn't have the same nine-to-five job, so why would they have the same roles and responsibilities when trying to create a Human Performance culture? But that's exactly what happens when most groups try to adopt Human Performance. Everyone in the organization attends the same seminar or completes the same computer-based training and walks away with the idea they have the same roles and responsibilities when it comes to adopting Human Performance. When this is the game plan, you've likely already lost the game.

Think of it in terms of an American football team. Everyone in the organization shares a clear goal: win games and win a championship. Different teams may have different strategies to accomplish this. Some may build their teams through the draft, while others rely on free agency. Some may feel that *defense wins championships*, while others think *the best defense is a good offense*. There are myriad systems, schemes, and philosophies that are the basis of a broader strategy for success. However, you wouldn't give everyone in the organization the same responsibility and expect team success.

For example, what if a football team decided, "This team would perform better if we were all faster. Let's focus on training to increase team speed." This tactic could greatly benefit a large part of the team. Running backs, wide receivers, defensive backs, linebackers, special teams coverage, and maybe even the mobile quarterback could all use an extra gear. Even those big-bodied linemen could benefit from quicker footwork and faster hand techniques. But do you really care about your equipment manager's 40-yard dash time? What about the coaches and trainers? Does their straight-line speed help the organization's goal of winning games? What about the General Manager or ownership? Does the owner need to go through cone and ladder drills alongside the players? Of course not.

To create a Human Performance culture, people with different responsibilities should have different roles and take different actions. However, what often happens is everyone is given a lesson on Human Performance Tools and Traps and left to figure out for themselves what they should be doing with this information as it relates to their role within the organization.

Workers and players, leaders and coaches, executives and owners, all have different roles but share the same goal of winning. The workers, just like the players on the field, tend to get the most attention but their performance is greatly impacted by the leaders and executives. Ignoring the role of management and upper leadership is probably why your previous performance improvement initiatives didn't stick. It was a bottom-up approach. Leaders didn't know how to coach it and executives didn't take ownership of it.

Think of the challenges your frontline leader is facing. If your organization is like most, you took your best worker and made them a leader. Being a good worker is a different skillset from being a good leader, but this person was promoted and asked to figure it out. It's like taking your fastest player and making them the Head Coach because they are really good at being fast, so maybe they'll be good at coaching.

This sounds insane but how often do you see the *super-doer* become the supervisor without the training and guidance they need?

Just as players, coaches, and managers have different roles in improving the performance of the team, your workers, leaders, and executives have different roles. Don't start an HP process thinking performance improvement is a one-size-fits all approach, as it's doomed to fail. Understand that your shared goal is accomplished when EVERYONE knows their distinct role and the unique actions they need to take to meet the larger team goals.

This is the concept behind the REMEDY Matrix; defining the different roles and responsibilities when it comes to creating a Human Performance culture.

The REMEDY Matrix is the graphical representation of an organization having a shared strategy (Human Performance culture) while defining individual tactics across three levels of the organization to support this goal. Different roles have different actions because each impacts the culture differently.

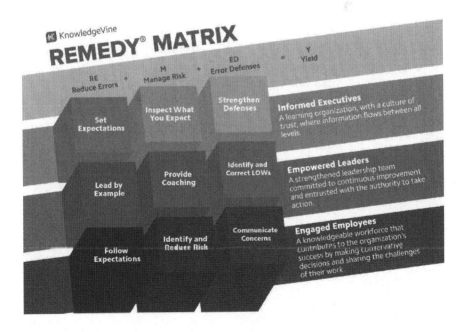

The matrix has the organization divided into three broad groups:

EXECUTIVES—upper management

LEADERS—front-line leadership

EMPLOYEES—individual contributors

Each of these groups has a different role in the day-to-day operations of an organization, and certainly has distinct responsibilities when it comes to Human Performance culture change. Each of the nine blocks of the REMEDY Matrix will be covered in greater detail in later chapters (remember, the trees) but for now, it's important to understand how the actions found in each block will influence the Culture Cycle to help create lasting change.

Think about the previous example of the football team. In this example the organization is broken down as such:

EXECUTIVE—Owner or General Manager

LEADERS—Coaches and Trainers

EMPLOYEES—Players

Now let's apply their roles to the goal of improving team speed.

	Set Expectations	Inspect What You Expect	Strengthen Defenses
Owner	Clearly set "team speed" as a priority and define the plans for this expectation.	Ensure the plan is being accurately executed as you defined it.	Measure progress and adjust tactics as needed to meet the larger goal.
Coach	**Lead by Example** Demonstrate ownership of the plan and start executing it.	**Provide Coaching** Help the players execute their required actions.	**Identify and Correct LOWs** Remove the impediments to the successful execution of the plan.
Player	**Follow Expectations** Understand and do your part to support the plan.	**Identify and Reduce Risk** Determine and remove the conditions that could put you at risk of failing to meet these expectations.	**Communicate Concerns** Let leadership know any challenges in executing the plan.

Owners set the plan. Coaches guide the plan. Players engage in the plan. Feedback is given and the necessary adjustments are made to improve the plan's success. Everyone has a shared goal, and everyone has their own roles and responsibilities to ensure this goal is met and sustained.

In this example, the strategy laid out in the REMEDY Matrix should make sense and it should be clear that it gives us a higher probability of success. Of course, most people aren't part of a football team, so let's look at an example a little closer to your work, such as the glove use requirement. As you recall there were many pitfalls with the all-to-familiar *here's a memo about glove use* process for change. We also shared how the Culture Cycle is not impacted in any sustainable way with one-and-done training. Finally, we identified the problems associated with one-size-fits-all strategies.

So how would the REMEDY Matrix approach a *glove use requirement* in order to have a sustainable impact on the culture? Let's take a high-level look at the process:

	Set Expectations	Inspect What You Expect	Strengthen Defenses
Executives	Clearly set "glove use" as a priority and define the plan for this expectation.	Go in the field and ensure the team is wearing gloves when required.	Validate and adjust the glove use requirement to ensure it's still appropriate.
Leaders	**Lead by Example** Demonstrate ownership and ensure the resources are in place.	**Provide Coaching** Coach the workers on proper glove use; provide positive reinforcement when needed.	**Identify and Correct LOWs** Fix the things that make glove use a challenge for the worker.
Employees	**Follow Expectations** Understand when to wear gloves and do it.	**Identify and Reduce Risk** Determine the conditions within your control that might discourage glove use.	**Communicate Concerns** Share what makes the glove use requirement difficult to follow.

You can see how clearly defined roles and responsibilities will have a greater impact on glove use compliance in the field. It's not just a memo outlining the behavior wanted and hoping for the best. It's knowing how the entire organization can influence the Culture Cycle to achieve these behaviors; even when no one is watching.

The actions in the REMEDY Matrix were not developed in a vacuum. They were designed to support Human Performance culture change by impacting the Culture Cycle. The following is an important concept that's critical to creating a Human Performance culture:

The REMEDY formula provides the broad strategy and REMEDY Matrix defines the tactics used to influence the Culture Cycle to create and sustain the Human Performance culture you desire.

Let's look at how the tactics in the REMEDY Matrix influence the Culture Cycle.

	Set Expectations	Inspect What You Expect	Strengthen Defenses
Executives	Clearly set "glove use" as a priority and define the plan for this expectation.	Go in the field and ensure the team is wearing gloves when required.	Validate and adjust the glove use requirement to ensure it's still appropriate.
Leaders	**Lead by Example** Demonstrate ownership and ensure the resources are in place.	**Provide Coaching** Coach the workers on proper glove use; provide positive reinforcement when needed.	**Identify and Correct LOWs** Fix the things that make glove use a challenge for the worker.
Employees	**Follow Expectations** Understand when to wear gloves and do it.	**Identify and Reduce Risk** Determine the conditions within your control that might discourage glove use.	**Communicate Concerns** Share what makes the glove use requirement difficult to follow.

When Executives *Set Expectations* and Leaders *Lead by Example* it influences the worker's belief in the appropriateness of the behaviors they need to exhibit. Even if they don't 100% buy in to the expectation, if they at least *Follow Expectations,* you are getting the behaviors you need until they do get on board.

Behaviors can be influenced in real-time when Executives are in the field to *Inspect What You Expect,* Leaders *Provide Coaching,* and Employees *Identify and Reduce Risk* by taking appropriate actions and helping others to follow suit. The results of these improved behaviors should be safe, accurate, efficient outcomes leading to a positive experience.

If not, the workers should *Communicate Concerns* and tell their leadership what was difficult for them in the field, or what made the experience unsatisfying. Leaders should address these concerns and *Identify and Correct LOWs* to give the worker a better experience and shape the belief that their efforts are worthwhile. Executives should

Strengthen Defenses in an effort to establish processes that influence the workers' experience and beliefs

Culture change is difficult and there have been several concepts and moving parts (some of the trees) presented in this chapter. Now might be a good time to remind you about the forest.

Human Performance reduces the frequency and severity of human error in the workplace. You want a Human Performance culture in your organization, but your current culture will fight you. You need to manage the culture change with a comprehensive plan that isn't one-and-done or one-size-fits-all. The REMEDY formula is the strategy for creating a Human Performance culture and the REMEDY Matrix is the tactics.

You have a goal and a plan with strategies and tactics for the entire organization. Before you look at a roadmap for implementing this plan, let's dissect one more issue that challenges organizational performance: If you don't know why people are making errors, how do you know the right steps to help them?

CHAPTER 4

WHY DID THIS HAPPEN?

"All highly competent people continually search for ways to keep learning, growing, and improving. They do that by asking WHY. After all, the person who knows HOW will always have a job, but the person who knows WHY will always be the boss."

~ Benjamin Franklin

As you've read this book, you no doubt have noticed several references to the success of the nuclear power industry, due in large part to their embracing of a Human Performance culture. If all you know about commercial nuclear power is Three Mile Island, Chernobyl, and Fukushima then it's understandable if you view these claims incredulously. So how good is commercial nuclear power?

According to the US Bureau of Labor Statistics, it's safer to show up to work every day at a nuclear power facility than any other job. Obviously, jobs like logging, commercial fishing, and agriculture don't set the bar very high, but commercial nuclear power is THE safest work environment by far. Working in a nuclear plant is safer than working in manufacturing, leisure and hospitality, real estate, or the financial sector.[4]

Skeptics will look at this obsession with safety and counter with, "If safety is the top priority, then productivity must take a backseat." This might be true if Human Performance only improved safety.

Human Performance is about consistency and accuracy to avoid mistakes. HP often gets discussed in terms of its impact on safety because the health and safety of our people is the top priority for all of us—and mandated by OSHA. However, avoiding errors also impacts quality, efficiency, and helps us avoid rework and time lost recovering from accidents. While nuclear power is the safest of all industries, it's also the most efficient of the energy sector producers.

The Capacity Factor is a measure of a generating plant's ability to produce maximum power over the course of the year. On average 92.5% of the time a nuclear plant is capable of operating at full capacity. If nuclear didn't have a Human Performance culture, these plants, with their highly technical and complex processes, would succumb to human error more frequently than they do. Events like operator error, plant trips, equipment failures due to faulty maintenance, or any other issues related to a lack of quality work, would result in nuclear having a Capacity Factor closer to that of their energy sector peers.[5]

None of this is intended to be a *pro nuclear energy* pitch. It's simply to point out that the US nuclear power industry has come the closest to cracking the code that allows industries to have incredible worker safety without compromising efficiency. So how does Human Performance help the nuclear power industry achieve this? Nuclear power, looking at every event through a Human Performance lens, does a phenomenal job of understanding where risks exist, asking why this risk is present, and taking action to prevent this risk from causing accidents and injuries.

Let's revisit the simple example of a glove use policy. Remember the advantages of having a comprehensive approach where you *set clear expectations, provide coaching, and inspect what you expect*; all the elements found in the REMEDY Matrix? Despite these types of efforts, a nuclear power plant might still find itself with a glove problem; after all, humans are fallible and even the best make mistakes. What they do about their glove problem is what separates their culture from others.

Here's the typical assessment of a glove use policy, which is usually precipitated by a series of hand injuries:

- Make glove use compliance a focus item.
- Leaders going into the field, sensitive to glove use compliance, will see people not wearing their gloves.

- Good leaders will engage with the violating worker to explain the importance of glove use and ask for cooperation with the rule.

- Less competent leaders will not engage the worker but will make a note and be sure to include it in the write up of their observation.

- These incidences get rolled up into a trend.

- At the end of the month the organization can cite the number of times gloves weren't utilized and email everyone about the need to improve glove usage.

- Optional—there's a stand-down to highlight the issue.

- Optional—ominous threats about "the next person caught..."

In any event, there may be a bump in glove use compliance as you have raised awareness about the issue and most workers will give more effort to comply to avoid being on any bad list.

Here's the problem that nuclear and aviation understand: *Awareness isn't usually the problem.*

Let's say there were 50 instances of glove violations noted over the last month. Do you think all 50 people didn't comply for the exact same reason; and that reason is awareness? Of course not. Think about the myriad reasons why someone would not wear gloves when they are required.

- Maybe they didn't know the requirement or have conflicting guidance causing confusion.

- Maybe they physically don't have access to gloves.

- Maybe they are never held accountable to the rules because leadership never goes into the field to see. There's a "rule" but it must be a low priority because nobody looks.

- Maybe their supervisor doesn't say anything when they see other workers without gloves, so it must not be that important.

- There's a rule but it feels unimportant and kind of optional because of implied consent.

- Maybe they have never had training on specific glove selection and use for a particular job and are just winging it.

- They know what to do but don't know how to do it.

- Maybe they just won't because they are insubordinate.

Then again, maybe they did just forget, and awareness is ONE answer but not the ONLY answer.

If there are 50 observations of non-compliance, then there are multiple reasons WHY. To treat all of these instances the same is misguided, unfair, and all too familiar. How unfair and ineffective is it to treat the worker who CAN'T do it because gloves aren't available, the same as the worker who just WON'T do it because they are insubordinate. Besides that, when all you do is send out an awareness reminder with a *we're serious this time* slant, neither the root cause of CAN'T nor WON'T is addressed at all! The reason this happens is because you looked at WHAT was missed but you never asked why. Without understanding WHY, you will seldom understand the cause, so you settle on the wrong solutions for the real issue.

Human Performance helps you understand it's not a glove problem. The glove problem is a symptom of the real issue. The real problem lies closer to the WHY. For example, if the reason WHY most workers are not using gloves is they CAN'T because gloves are not readily available, then it might be a storeroom or supply chain issue. The symptom of CAN'T could just as easily show up in not using safety glasses or other Personal Protective Equipment (PPE) that is also in short supply. If workers had better access to job materials it would solve a wide range of issues, not just the glove problem.

What if the reason WHY is they didn't know they SHOULD? This could be a training or communication issue. If they don't know when they SHOULD wear gloves, what else are they missing? Look at how you set expectations for how all work is performed, not just glove requirements.

What if the reason WHY is they don't know HOW? This could be a coaching or training issue. Look at how you develop your people to equip them with the skills to do their work.

What if the reason WHY is the person just WON'T? What else have you asked that they just aren't doing? Now you might be headed toward remediation or progressive discipline to solve this problem.

Nuclear and aviation are obsessed with answering the question, "Why did this happen?" When they understand this, they take steps to solve the root cause.

> *Instead of putting out 50 "they aren't wearing gloves" fires, they find the source of the sparks and eliminate that.*

Think about how solving for WHY works within the Culture Cycle. Understanding and addressing WHY will influence the worker's beliefs and experience. If the worker believes they aren't accountable because no one ever looks, then go in-field and *Inspect What You Expect* to shift this belief. If the worker's experience is frustrating because they want to comply but CAN'T due to a lack of resources, then provide the resources to remove this frustration and create a positive experience. If the worker doesn't know HOW to do it, provide training to shape their beliefs in their ability. To have a lasting impact, these influences on the Culture Cycle need to be a continuous process. Just as *awareness* can have a temporary impact before you drift back into old habits, the influence of solving for the WHY will also start to wane as soon as you take your focus off it. Understand WHY and solve that problem; not the symptom of WHAT was missed.

With all the varying reasons each person might not follow a rule or expectation, it might be difficult to trend a reason WHY. If asked to suppose why a worker's behaviors didn't match the standard, you could probably rattle off a few examples without too much effort; didn't know they were supposed to, simply forgot, physically can't, etc. If you get too specific with the WHY then you could lose the ability to spot a trend. For example, specific reasons like, "I thought Steve was doing it," "I didn't know I was supposed to," or "Nobody told me," might seem like three different reasons but are all actually rooted in the same, "I didn't know I should" reason WHY.

To get closer to the root cause you need some organization to the data you are collecting; some broad categories to help spot trends. If you just asked why every time, with no strategy for collecting data, you would likely end up with some scattered, unorganized, and unactionable information. To help bring some organization to this, KnowledgeVine uses the nine most common reasons our thousands of interactions have revealed for WHY workers fail to comply with expectations. For simplicity's sake, we have them listed here:

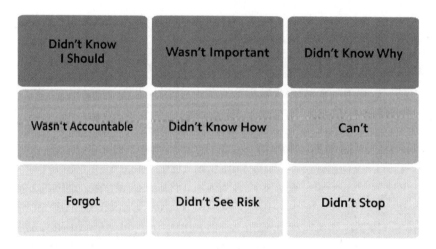

You can probably infer what each of these means, but to avoid the trap of *Vague Guidance*, the following provides a little more context:

DIDN'T KNOW I SHOULD: Didn't know there was an expectation/rule/policy or Vague Guidance about this rule created confusion. This might be a communication problem.

WASN'T IMPORTANT: Workers know there's a rule, but it seems optional since leadership doesn't follow it themselves or never says anything when they see others not doing it. There might be a problem of creating implied consent or tacit approval.

DIDN'T KNOW WHY: Workers were told to do it but the reasons for doing it were never explained, so everyone lacks buy-in and commitment which leads to inconsistent compliance. This might be a training issue.

WASN'T ACCOUNTABLE: Although there's a rule, workers have the option to not follow it because leadership never checks to see if it's happening. There might be a problem with a lack of employee oversight.

DIDN'T KNOW HOW: Workers are aware of the general rule but haven't been given the coaching or training to understand the specific technical actions they should be taking. Might be a coaching problem.

CAN'T: Workers physically cannot follow the rule due to physical constraints, a lack of equipment, materials, resources, procedures, or other guidance. This might be a gap in how the organization structures work.

FORGOT: As simple as a memory lapse. Workers know the rule to follow but it just slipped their mind. It might be a situational awareness problem. Note: When talking with workers "Forgot" is often offered but not likely the reason. Workers often say, "I forgot" in an effort to quickly end the discussion. Leaders involved in this discussion need to ask "why the worker forgot" to get closer to the root cause. Did they truly forget or just never considered it due to one of the other eight WHYS ?

DIDN'T SEE RISK: Workers didn't think there was any risk based on their experience and knowledge, or they were unaware of the risk due to not paying attention or being distracted. Basically, they didn't look, or they looked and missed it.

DIDN'T STOP: While engaged in the task, workers failed to recognize drifting conditions, scope change or elements of the plan that will no longer work. Workers failed to stop and communicate these changes with leadership, resulting in an error or noncompliance with the rule. There might be an issue with stop work authority, near miss reporting, or the ability and comfort of workers to report issues.

Think about how this insight could help you better respond to the previous example of the glove issue. Instead of having 50 observations of workers not wearing gloves and putting out those fires with *awareness* communications, you can now target the source of sparks because you have a better idea of the root cause, or WHY. If 30 workers shared that they don't have access to gloves, then you have a CAN'T issue to tackle and need to validate if workers have the resources to meet expectations. If ten workers state they simply forgot, then those workers need coaching and tools to help increase their focus or situational awareness. If ten said they didn't know they SHOULD, then some *awareness* communication might be part of the solution—as long as it's in conjunction with reviewing the effectiveness of your other communications and guidelines to assess what else the worker may not know.

Keep in mind, the discussion here isn't about finding the root cause after an accident or injury. This is about trending the behaviors of your workers to identify risk taking to avoid costly errors. While you should certainly look at why you had an event post-accident or injury, the discussion here is centered around risky precursor behaviors.

Most discussion about precursor behaviors involves those risks that preceded a negative result; looking backwards at what happened and using this information to prevent recurrence. This is certainly advisable to prevent the next event, but if you don't have robust near miss reporting or an effective observation process to spot risk-taking trends, then most of your learning will come post-accident. You certainly can't ignore the lessons learned from accidents past, but if you can start to *identify risky behaviors that are not aligned with your standards BEFORE an event*, you can arrest and turn this negative trend and avoid the costly price of an accident or injury.

To identify risk, you need to know where it is created.

Most risk is found in the gap between your Standards (work as directed) and your Behaviors (work as performed).

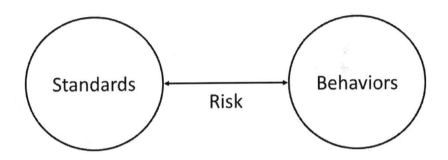

There's a great deal of talk around this topic. You may have heard it described as _work imagined vs work realized_ or _work as prescribed vs work as performed._ What we are trying to convey with all this is simply the concept that risk is created when there is a gap between the standards and behaviors. You have a work standard, like the glove requirement, but when gloves aren't worn, the behaviors aren't aligned with the standard, creating risk. The more often workers adhere to the standard, the closer aligned behaviors are with the standard, and the less risk you have. Pretty simple.

However, knowing Human Performance isn't only about the individual, then you also understand that the organization can create risk by having faulty or misapplied standards. Sometimes the standards are inadequate which creates risk the employee must work around to get work done. The standard could be difficult to apply to the actual work. The standard could be poorly communicated and unclear. The standard could be unenforced, not coached, not demonstrated by leadership, or just plain wrong for the type of work that employees perform. When the standards are misaligned with work in the field, this also creates risk for the worker to navigate.

Highly reliable organizations do a great job of ensuring that standards are aligned with behaviors. You can be assured of two things that happen in nuclear and aviation:

1) Workers seldom deviate from the standard.

2) The standards are correct so there's no reason to deviate.

Find the risk existing between your standards and your actual behaviors, then start understanding WHY it is there.

Nuclear and aviation have the Human Performance cultures in place that drive them toward always seeking to understand WHY there is risk BEFORE an accident, injury, or error; and not just WHAT happened post event. They recognize that risky *precursor behaviors* can be trended to drive organizations to high standards; not just to avoid recurrence of undesired results. This allows them to eliminate the source of the sparks and stop continually putting out fires.

This might seem like a lofty or unattainable goal. After all, nuclear and aviation have the benefit of a several decade head start and have established organizational structures that have grown to support this approach to the point where they now have staff strictly dedicated to Human Performance improvement. However, if you don't get started then you'll never make progress toward benefiting from a Human Performance culture. The good news is, you're reading this book, so you are already getting started, but let's back up and look at the ground you have covered so far.

To this point, you've absorbed a great deal of information:

- The Culture Cycle and how it can be influenced to create the organizational culture you desire.

- Human Performance, in general, and how it is helping industries like nuclear power and aviation to be the safest, most efficient industries.

- The REMEDY formula as a specific strategy to create a Human Performance culture

- The REMEDY Matrix helps define the roles and responsibilities of each person in creating this culture, since one-size doesn't fit all.

- Understanding that risk exists in the gap between standards and behaviors.

- Seeking to understand WHY you're getting the behaviors you're getting to help you identify risky precursor behaviors before an event.

There are a multitude of good concepts and strategies involved in these previous discussions and individually they each make inherent sense. Next, let's see how all of this information fits together in easy-to-understand actionable steps.

BRINGING IT ALL INTO FOCUS

CHAPTER 5

"The only thing that can grow is the thing you give energy to."

~ Ralph Waldo Emerson (1803 – 1883)

With decades of experience in nuclear power and the military, KnowledgeVine's leadership brings the same mentality to helping organizations create a Human Performance culture. Because of this, it's no accident that there are nine WHYs and also nine boxes in the REMEDY Matrix. Each reason WHY can be traced to a weakness or failure in a REMEDY Matrix focus area. For example, if workers don't know they *should* do something, it's likely a failure of upper management to Set Expectations clearly. If the worker doesn't know *how* to do something, it's likely a failure to Provide Coaching. If the worker *won't*, then it's a failure of the individual to Support Change. If the worker saw the risk but didn't stop, then it's a failure to Communicate Concerns.

Executives	**Set Expectations** Didn't Know I Should	**Inspect What You Expect** Wasn't Important	**Strengthen Defenses** Didn't Know Why
Leaders	**Lead by Example** Wasn't Accountable	**Provide Coaching** Didn't Know How	**Identify and Correct LOWs** Can't
Employees	**Follow Expectations** Forgot	**Identify and Reduce Risk** Didn't See Risk	**Communicate Concerns** Didn't Stop

With all these tactics it might be a good time to work our way back to the 10,000-foot view of the KnowledgeVine brand of Human Performance to remind ourselves about the strategy this all supports. The chart above lays out the relationship between WHY you might be getting the wrong behaviors, what part of the REMEDY Matrix is lacking, and how you might target a better solution as opposed to a shotgun approach.

The following chart illustrates how all the elements work together to improve performance and shape the culture.

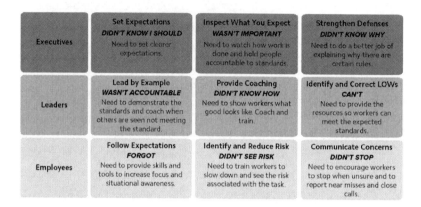

The REMEDY Matrix lays out the different roles and responsibilities for creating a Human Performance culture, and you can also see the part each person plays in setting up workers for success or their roles in correcting behaviors that don't meet the standards and expectations. Keep in mind these roles and responsibilities aren't just about safety. If Executives, Leaders, and Employees are all doing their part, quality and efficiency will also increase in other areas of the work.

You have read how the Culture Cycle needs to be influenced in the right direction to shift and create the culture you need. You can see how engagement from different levels of the organization can have an influence on beliefs, behaviors, results, and experiences. We looked at a couple of examples earlier, but actions like *Set Expectations* or *Lead by Example will* influence beliefs. Actions like *Inspect What You Expect, Provide Coaching, Follow Expectations,* and *Identify and Reduce Risk* can all have an impact on behaviors as engagement is happening where the critical behaviors are occurring. Actions like *Strengthen Defenses, Identify and Correct LOWs,* and *Communicate Concerns* should demonstrate for the worker that positive change is occurring. This is an encouraging result and a positive experience that feeds back into their beliefs and the cycle continues.

How about risk? You learned how risk is created when the worker doesn't adhere to the standards or when the standards are insufficient for the work being performed. Understanding why is important, so you can take targeted actions to address the real issue and not just react by raising awareness. Trending the WHYs is important to find the root causes. Knowing this will help your team see the difference between a vague *glove* problem and a *can't, forgot, or didn't know I should* problem.

Looking at how this all ties together, you may be asking, "What happened to the REMEDY Formula?" Let's look at how this is layered into the process as well.

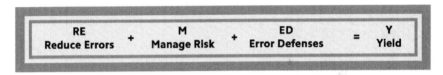

Remember the elements of the REMEDY Formula:

RE—Reduce Errors. Eliminating those active, in-the-moment, individual errors. Things like grabbing the wrong switch, operating the wrong breaker, closing the wrong valve, or capturing the wrong information. Usually, the triggering action of an event or accident, but not the only cause.

M—Manage Risk. Identifying risk may be an individual effort, but effectively managing this risk requires a team approach. Everyone must do their part to mitigate risks whether that is observing the work in the field, providing proper guidance through coaching, or identifying the risk and making a conservative decision about the next step. You should strive to mitigate risks in all areas, whether it is a change in the existing processes, a deviation in the work plan, or a questionable piece of equipment that might lead to unwanted circumstances.

ED—Error Defenses. Understanding that the organization and work structures have an enormous influence on the worker's behaviors. Are you setting workers up for success by defending against errors or asking them to overcome error likely situations?

Y—Yield. If individuals can reduce active errors, errors, identify and control risks, and strengthen error defenses to give them the best chance for success, it will create an organization that is resilient against human error.

Now let's look at how the REMEDY Matrix provides the tactics for creating a Human Performance culture by defining the roles and responsibilities in support of the REMEDY Formula:

RE: Reduce Error—Eliminating Active Errors

SET EXPECTATIONS

Executives set clear expectations for the use of Human Performance.

LEAD BY EXAMPLE

Leaders demonstrate their commitment by using Human Performance themselves and holding their teams accountable to the same.

FOLLOW EXPECTATIONS

Employees utilize the Human Performance training and tools they were provided to increase their focus and prevent active errors.

M: Manage Risk—Identifying and Controlling Risk

Inspect What You Expect

Executives show their commitment to Human Performance by going in the field to ensure expectations are being met.

Provide Coaching

Leaders provide real-time coaching to their teams to use Human Performance.

Identify and Reduce Risk

Employees understand the impact of their actions and make decisions considering unwanted circumstances.

ED: Error Defenses—Fixing The Issues That Challenge Worker Performance.

This is mostly about identifying LATENT ORGANIZATIONAL WEAKNESSES and correcting the conditions that set workers up for failure. Since workers have the best view of what is broken, let's work this one from their level up.

Communicate Concerns

Employees need to stop and report when conditions make it difficult for them to complete their work per the established standards.

Identify And Correct LOWs (Latent Organizational Weaknesses)

Leaders need to help employees identify LOWs and need to take actions to correct the conditions that challenge workers.

STRENGTHEN DEFENSES

> Executives use data to understand why gaps exist between standards and behaviors and put processes in place to minimize this gap.

At this point it should be clearer how the REMEDY Formula, as a strategy, and the REMEDY Matrix, as tactics, work to influence the Culture Cycle to create a Human Performance culture. You should start to have a vision of what good looks like and where you want to go. However, in the introduction we promised more. We also want you to understand HOW you are going to establish a Human Performance culture. In other words, what are the strategies and tactics for rolling out a process to your people?

In the introduction we presented a rough outline of the book, the forest, and the trees. We also introduced a set of questions to consider preventing your Human Performance initiative from becoming the latest in a line of programs to come and go.

- Why do bad things keep happening? (Human Error)
- Where can we turn to stop Human Error? (Human Performance)
- Where are we now? (Understand the current culture)
- What is the path forward? (What does "good" look like)
- How do we keep the momentum going? (Prevent drift and keep improving)
- What does each person need to do to accomplish all of the above?

The reason for revisiting these issues is twofold. First, it's a good time to check our progress and to take a moment to recognize the ground covered before moving on. Second, let's recognize where we've been so we can differentiate that from where we are going as we progress further. Some of the previous bullets have been covered in detail, some have been touched on to tee up further discussions, and some still need to be explored. To help you get a lay of the land to this point, let's review where you are in the forest.

THE FOREST

What Has Been Covered

Know what you're up against by understanding the strength and importance of organizational culture.

Look at how individuals are simultaneously creating the culture while also being influenced by it.

Learn the broad strategy for creating a Human Performance culture.

Understand how each level of the organization can start working together toward the common goal of creating a Human Performance culture.

Still To Come

Develop a change management strategy with Human Performance in mind.

You now have a view of the forest that includes understanding culture, influencing culture, a strategy for Human Performance, and roles and responsibilities to make it happen.

You know where you want to go.

What remains is developing a change management strategy with Human Performance in mind, so you know how to get there.

Let's explore a change management strategy next.

REMEDY®

CHAPTER 6

DIAS ROADMAP

"It isn't what you do, but how you do it."

~ John Wooden (1910 – 2010)

As you recall, the failures during the construction of the Spanish S-80 Plus submarine, the Isaac Peral, could be traced back to a single, misplaced decimal point by an engineer. This triggered a series of ensuing errors as the team tried to react and adjust. It's not often you can look back and find the first domino that fell. Usually, it's a series of events that combine in a perfect storm to spell the demise of a program. A good example of this is the Ford Edsel. It wasn't one error that doomed the Edsel, but rather it was a series of tactical mistakes.[6]

You could write an entire book on the lessons learned from the failure of the Edsel, and several people have. To keep the conversation succinct, here is a quick overview of some of the things that went wrong.

MISREADING WHAT PEOPLE NEED: Ford thought consumers wanted an upscale car when buyers were actually moving towards more economical vehicles.

NOT GETTING BUY-IN BEFORE EXECUTING: In an effort to build the suspense, Ford kept details about the Edsel secret and didn't conduct enough market research to learn that people didn't want the Edsel.

CONFUSED PROCESS: The Edsel had four series, in eighteen models, with six body styles and two wheelbase options. It was overwhelming.

LACK OF DISTINCTION: The Edsel borrowed hardware from other Ford models and was priced similarly to other vehicles in their fleet. It didn't seem different enough for consumers to warrant taking a chance on this brand-new car.

45

MANAGEMENT MISALIGNMENT: The leadership at Ford was divided on the concept of the Edsel. A lack of clear, unified commitment led to siloed thinking and tactical decisions being made in a vacuum, hastening Ford's cancellation of the Edsel after just two years.

POOR QUALITY: The car was designed with some innovative ideas. On paper, these ideas looked great. In application, it didn't work, and the car was unreliable.

POOR DESIGN: Culture is a powerful thing. Once the problems started piling up, the Edsel became a joke and the label of "ugly and unreliable" easily stuck. They couldn't give away the cars and had to offer rebates to those who had previously bought one.

When it comes to executing a plan, it's crucial to have a solid roadmap. The Edsel was supposed to change the landscape of the car industry, but a lack of planning and execution prevented Ford from having the kind of impact they desired. In fact, the failure of the Edsel did a great deal of damage to Ford's reputation and cost the company $250 million dollars; the equivalent of $2.5 billion today. If Ford had to do it over again, they probably wouldn't do it at all.

Similarly, the potential damage that could be done by trying and failing to implement a Human Performance culture is a big reason why many organizations won't even try. Better to leave it alone and hope for the best, rather than take two steps backwards if it doesn't have the impact you desired. The risk is too great for many managers since a failed Human Performance rollout can also have reputational and monetary costs within their company. To mitigate this risk, you need a roadmap that avoids the type of pitfalls that beset the plans for the Ford Edsel. A roadmap that considers:

READING THE CURRENT LANDSCAPE and knowing what your people need.

GETTING EMPLOYEE BUY-IN and being transparent before pushing forward.

CONFIRMING YOUR TEAM clearly understands the plan.

KEEPING IT SIMPLE so no one gets overwhelmed.

SHOWING THEM WHAT GOOD LOOKS LIKE and how it's different from business as usual.

GETTING MANAGEMENT ALIGNMENT and ensuring their continued commitment and support.

NOT GRABBING THE CHEAPEST, LOWEST QUALITY HP PROCESS to "check the box."

GIVING YOUR PEOPLE A QUALITY HP PROCESS that works for them in application and not just in theory.

If you try and fail, the culture will kick in and label all *Human Performance* processes as *ugly and unreliable*. Any subsequent efforts will have a higher hill to climb; so get it right the first time.

You have a goal, now get the right roadmap so you don't drive Human Performance into the ditch.

The goal: create a Human Performance culture in your organization. While goals are great, they will remain lofty ambitions without a plan for moving it forward. As you may have witnessed for yourself, or at least recognized in the failure of the Edsel, any new process that is just thrown out there without any change management is likely going to fail. "In fact, according to Forbes Magazine, 70% of all change initiatives will fail." [7] Keep in mind, these are just the groups that reported they tried and failed. There's no telling how many organizations looked at these long odds and didn't even try, or how many didn't report their failure. As stated earlier, your culture will fight you; and wins 70% of the time.

The Edsel isn't the only cautionary tale of an organization to set a goal and haphazardly deployed a solution without giving enough consideration to the implementation plan to ensure its success. Likewise, there are many groups offering solutions to help you avoid this trap. If you Google search *change management*, there is no shortage of

"Seven Steps to Organizational Change" or "Four Pitfalls of Change Management" results. It's interesting reading that often becomes a postmortem of your last failed initiative as you recognize what may have been missed in hindsight.

It's great that there is a wealth of information available, but it can be overwhelming. Each change management strategy has a little twist or different emphasis. Some guidance seems spot-on while others may appear to be a forced fit for your organization. Are Eight simple steps better than seven? How much strategy is too much?

Additionally, some change management processes will work well if you're trying to roll out a new payroll system for your employees but might not be great if you're retooling the assembly line for a new product; and certainly not a great fit for something as hard to define as organizational culture. It's easy to get stuck at the starting line with what is called analysis paralysis. Too many options can be a bad thing.

Initially, KnowledgeVine struggled with this same issue. We wanted to answer the question, "What is the broad change management strategy that's easiest to deploy and fits the most organizations?" We found the literature too widely varying in its guidance. From our time in nuclear, we had learned many of the tactics that helped ensure the success and longevity of culture change efforts but had never really considered how all of this fit into a broader strategy, if we were missing anything, and, most importantly, how could we structure this strategy to be applicable to other organizations.

As we looked at our process that had naturally evolved, we looked to align these tactics with a change management strategy that would make culture change efforts easier, and DIAS emerged.

DIAS is our acronym for our culture change management process. Each element will be discussed in greater detail in the subsequent chapters but broadly, DIAS stands for:

Discover

Inform

Apply

Sustain

As a change management strategy for your culture, it's easy to understand, widely applicable, and creates the roadmap needed to ensure your efforts fall into that elusive 25% of change initiatives that work. You need to DISCOVER where you are as an organization, be INFORMED about where you want to go, learn how to APPLY this information to create change, and then SUSTAIN this momentum until you reach your goal. Again, there are many tactics involved in each phase of the DIAS culture change strategy but...

Knowing "who you are now—who you want to be—how you start doing it—and how you keep doing it" is crucial for your success.

Think of your Human Performance culture change as a journey. As with any trip, you need to know where you want to go, where you are, how you're going to get there, start taking steps in the right direction, and keep the momentum going until you arrive.

For example, the family has decided, for whatever reason, to take a vacation to Disney World™ this summer. Where you want to go has been decided, so what are the tactics for getting there? Well first, you need to know where you are before you can start in any direction. This may seem obvious, and we don't give a lot of thought to it since our physical location is easy to define and understand. However, not understanding your current culture, and trying to start changing it, is as ill-advised as randomly heading due west to get to Disney World. It's not going to get most people there, unless you happen to live in Titusville, Florida (Don't look it up...it's directly east of Orlando.) Discover where you are before you start taking steps.

Now that you have taken the time to DISCOVER where you are, it might seem like the next steps are pretty easy. Let's hop in the car and head to Disney World. Again, you are probably taking for granted how easy it is to drive a car since you have a lot of experience with it. Adopting Human Performance is a lot like learning to drive a car; it's new and unfamiliar at first but with enough practice, it can become second nature and very efficient. Going in with the assumption that your team is going to easily adopt Human Performance behaviors is about as fair to the worker as insisting that your six-year-old suddenly learn how to drive and safely navigate the family on this Disney trip. This is a huge change management pitfall—assuming everyone has your level of understanding and proficiency of this new process.

Similar to driving a car, this new Human Performance behavior needs to be learned, coached, and practiced. The first phase of becoming a driver is being INFORMED about the rules of the road, as well as the theories and methods of vehicle operation. There's training and information to set expectations and create a vision of what safe driving looks like; hopefully, you didn't just jump behind the wheel with no training when you learned to drive. You had coaching and instruction.

While the driving knowledge gained is critically important, you need to APPLY that knowledge to the act of driving, otherwise you haven't moved out of the driveway. However, you don't expect someone to learn the skills of driving, give them a license, and send them on their way. First, you get a permit and practice driving under supervision. This is another pitfall in implementing a Human Performance process; most don't recognize the need to have a learning curve, or *learner's permit*. Think about the last time your organization tried to implement change. Did it go something like, "Here's some training on the new process. Any questions? No? Go get 'em!" While there may have been some constructive feedback as everyone stumbled through their own idea of how to meet expectations, there wasn't any proactive coaching while everyone learned the ropes. Ideally, your new driver should have some time to APPLY safe driving techniques before hitting the interstate system for hours of driving.

So, you decided to go to Disney, determined where you were, didn't take for granted that everyone knew how to drive, trained and coached your drivers, and now you're headed toward Orlando. How do you ensure you make it all the way there? Some are comfortable with, "Let's see how far we can get, and we'll figure out rest, meals, and fuel along the way." Others prefer to schedule each leg of the trip and pre-determine all the pitstops. While planning and preparing is always the safest option, both groups are now making progress down the road.

Think about your last road trip to somewhere you have never been with people who haven't been there either, especially children. How quickly did your passengers get bored? If you weren't continuously reinforcing the vision of, "It'll be great!" or "You're gonna love it," there's a chance that members of your group would just as soon turn around and go back; and this is a trip they initially *wanted* to go on. Imagine if this road trip was to a destination, they never really got excited about in the first place and were pretty much along for the ride. They are looking for the first opportunity to turn around and go back to business as usual.

To SUSTAIN the momentum created, you need to continuously reinforce the vision of your goal and the expectations on how you are going to get there. "You're doing fantastic with driving, and you're going to get there safely and on time, which is great because I hear it's the happiest place on earth." This is, of course, an oversimplification of a culture change journey but the idea still holds. You must continuously remind everyone of the expectations, reinforce the right behaviors, coach on the wrong behaviors, and champion benefits of the Human Performance culture goal, otherwise they'll just want to go back.

DISCOVER where you are as an organization so you can head in the right direction.

INFORM your team about where you are going and tactics for getting there.

APPLY this information to start the organization moving down the road.

SUSTAIN this momentum to beat the odds and ensure you arrive at your goal.

Now it could be argued that culture change and continuous improvement is a journey, not a destination, so you never really arrive; and that's true. However, barring some weird scenario, Disney World is never the final destination either. It's one part of your journey. Maybe the next phase is a visit to Universal Studios™ or Sea World™. How easy is THAT trip since you're already in Orlando? Maybe you're headed back home, wiser for the experience and better prepared for whatever is next, though probably a little lighter in the wallet. You've learned what works and what doesn't, and that can inform and improve your next family road trip no matter where you go. Whatever the next significant phase of your culture improvement journey is, you can use DIAS to successfully get you there, and hopefully not in a Ford Edsel.

DISCOVERY

*If I were given one hour to save the planet, I would spend
59 minutes defining the problem and one minute
resolving it."*

~ Albert Einstein (1879 – 1955)

Kodak Photography company filed for bankruptcy in 2012. For a century, Kodak led the photography market and was the innovator behind the move from dry plates to film and from black and white to color photos. The demise of Kodak, along with Blockbuster or Blackberry, are well-known cautionary tales about organizations that failed to adapt to a changing marketplace and were left in the dustbin of corporate history. In Kodak's case, they were too late to adopt the digital camera. By the time Kodak realized the market was moving away from film and toward digital cameras, they were already out positioned by companies like Canon, Sony, and Nikon.

The fall of Kodak is a familiar story, especially if you were around to witness its collapse. Most people know that Kodak was killed by the digital camera, but did you know that Kodak invented the digital camera? Kodak engineer and R&D worker, Steve Sasson, invented the digital camera technology for Kodak in the late 1970's. Kodak shelved the technology out of fear that the technology was a direct competitor to the future of their film business; and they were right. Where Kodak failed is in recognizing the incredible opportunity the digital camera presented; and they owned the technology. Just as Dr. Frankenstein was killed by his own monster, Kodak was killed by a product of its own innovation.

The cautionary tale of Kodak is a reminder that the path to where you want to be tomorrow is heavily influenced by opportunities and challenges of where you are today. Before you embark on a journey

(Chapter 7 indicated in the left margin as "CHAPTER 7")

toward a Human Performance culture it's important to understand the current landscape of your organization.

There are many ways to Discover your organization's culture.

You could choose to have interviews with a sample of your workforce to gauge their attitudes. You could perform a series of jobsite observations to see the behaviors of your team over time. Customer feedback will give you insight into how others see your organization. KnowledgeVine prefers to implement an anonymous Culture Survey with a client's entire workforce. Not only will this help you read the pulse of the organization, but it serves as the first piece of data and sets a baseline for your company to measure progress against.

There are many advantages of the using a Culture Survey to Discover the culture of the organization. First, it's anonymous. This is more revealing than an interview or work observation when everyone is on their best behavior and possibly trying to give you what they think you want. You want to know the culture of the organization; they want to not make waves. Observations and interviews don't reveal the actual culture of the organization, they only show the culture of the organization when someone is watching.

Second, an anonymous survey is a great way to start getting the team involved in the culture change process. We often say to leadership, "We want to ask your people how they feel before we ask them for their effort." This may sound a little touchy-feely, but if your first introduction to Human Performance is, "Hey, go take this training," then the process has started without the team's engagement and feels forced upon them, setting you up for resistance.

Third, there is a critical piece of data that emerges from the survey that is the most predictive of your odds of successfully implementing a

Human Performance process; and it's not found in the survey questions themselves. Before the survey is distributed, we ask the upper leadership (President, CEO, owner, etc.) to send a message to the organization explaining what it is and personally asking for their participation. We set a target of 80% of the organization to complete the survey within the allotted time, which is usually two weeks. The groups that hit their 80% mark on time are the ones most likely to be successful moving forward. The groups that need to extend the time to get to 80% tend to struggle. The groups that never get above 50% usually make no discernable progress at all.

Think about how telling the participation rates are. Your CEO has told everyone in the organization how important it is to complete a 10-minute, online, anonymous survey. If the apathy in your organization is so bad that over half of your workforce won't do something as simple as completing a survey, then there are real problems within the culture. As our Founder David Bowman often says, "If your team won't do a survey the CEO asked them to do, what else are they not doing? Following safe work practices? Using PPE? Utilizing procedures? How can you lead them to improvement if they already aren't following you?"

If you can get good participation in the survey, then the results of the individual questions can be very revealing. The Culture Survey helps our clients to identify where the potential Latent Organizational Weaknesses (LOWs) and strengths are. Once everyone in the organization has taken the survey, we then mine the data for useful information. The results of the survey are a compilation of your team's beliefs. We simply hold a mirror up to your organization, showing you what it looks like. Through this lens, we are able to consult with our clients and point out areas for additional training and coaching during field visits. This is how you can get a better feel for the climate and practices within your organization. The survey is your discovery into the culture of your organization.

For example, do your workers feel like their leadership understands the challenges they face every day? Odds are your leaders think they understand this, and your workers think they don't. In fact this is one of the items in our Culture Survey and typically is one of the most disagreed-with.

There is much more detail on the survey in Section II (the trees), covering each of these items that are included in the survey.

The following are the statements from the survey:

- The company always looks for ways to improve how work is done.
- Employees are receptive to changes in the organization.
- Leaders actively develop employees by providing specific, constructive feedback.
- Employees conduct their work activities the same way, whether they are being observed or not.
- Safety is the top priority at our company.
- Activities are observed by someone in authority other than the direct supervisor.
- Executives anticipate problems and take actions to prevent them.
- Leaders never encourage anyone to bypass the rules.
- Leaders seek to understand the employee's point of view.
- Leaders quickly resolve issues.
- Employees follow the company rules.
- Employees think it is important to report all problems or close calls right away.
- Employees are receptive to coaching, and often coach each other.
- The company has established clear, written standards and expectations.

- Executives ensure company goals will be met by observing work activities.
- The company has a formal process in place to correct identified problems.
- Leaders model the right behaviors and lead by example.
- Leaders hold employees accountable to standards and expectations.
- Leaders have the authority to correct issues that impact job performance.
- Employees believe every task can be done without error or injury.
- The company is good at resolving problems.
- Employee development and training are important to the company.
- Leaders act in a way that reflects the company's values.
- Leaders encourage employees to identify and report work-related issues.
- Employees perform work tasks in a controlled, deliberate manner.
- Employees will not hesitate to stop a coworker if they think their actions are incorrect.
- When employees are unsure about a task, it is OK to stop.
- The company's goals are routinely communicated to all employees.
- Executives understand the challenges and concerns facing the workforce.
- Executives are always looking for ways to improve the company.
- Leaders clearly communicate their expectations.
- Leaders provide positive reinforcement of proper behaviors.
- When an event occurs, the company takes the right actions to make sure it doesn't happen again.
- Employees are trained in the use of error-reduction techniques.

- The actions of employees support the company's success.
- Employees are comfortable challenging existing conditions.

Discovering the pulse of your organization is crucial to understanding *where you are* before you embark on any new journey. The Culture Survey is one way to help you understand this. The hope is that you can glean some insight into this overall process, take what works for you, and apply it to your organization. As mentioned earlier, there are other methods you can use to discover the pulse of your culture, like interviews or observations, but it's important to give some effort to understanding your culture before you introduce a new process. Remember, you are trying to influence the Culture Cycle to get the results you ultimately want—an organization with a functioning Human Performance culture. You can best know how to influence the Culture Cycle if you truly understand the current beliefs you need to shape.

Remember, not all information gleaned from the discovery into your organization's culture is negative. You can find areas in your culture where your team excels and leverage this to help create the change you need.

Just as Kodak failed to recognize the enormous advantage they had in owning digital photography technology, your organization should be careful not to ignore its strengths.

If you find your culture is good at the concept of *Set Expectations,* then you probably already have a good process for explaining and documenting what needs to be done. If you find your culture is good at the concept of *Strengthen Defenses,* then you may already be adept at adopting new improvement processes. If your culture is good at the *Provide Coaching* concept, then let the Leader level of the organization take the point in the implementation of this new Human Performance initiative. If your employees can *Identify and Reduce Risk*, then make sure this strength is not minimized as new employees join the organization. Ensure new employees are aware that "this is the way it is done here" through their interactions with your Engaged Employees."

In any event, knowing *where you are* can help you better see the opportunities that lie in front of you or spot the challenges that may resist change. Create the vision of *where you want to be* and recognize the strengths within your organization that can help you to get there.

CHAPTER 8

INFORM

"An investment in knowledge always pays the best interest."

~ Benjamin Franklin (1706 – 1790)

August 21, 2017, the USS John S. McCain (DDG-56), a guided-missile destroyer, collided with a merchant ship off the coast of Singapore. The incident resulted in the death of 10 US Navy sailors. It's not often that US Navy ships collide with other vessels, however this incident came less than three months after the USS Fitzgerald struck a container ship off the coast of Japan, killing seven US Navy sailors.

In the immediate aftermath of the USS McCain collision, the US Navy suggested that a fatigued crew, poor crew communications, and crowded shipping lanes were the cause of the accident. Leadership was relieved of their duties due to a lack of confidence in their ability to command. However, a subsequent investigation by the National Transportation Safety Board (NTSB) took it a step further. The NTSB cited a "lack of effective operational oversight of the destroyer by the US Navy, which resulted in insufficient training and inadequate bridge operating procedures." [8]

Without getting too complicated, here's what the NTSB found. One person, the Helmsman, was controlling the speed AND steering of the ship. As they approached the busy shipping channel, the crew attempted to split the speed and steering responsibilities between the Helmsman and the Lee Helmsman. (The Lee Helmsman is like the assistant Helmsman.) The reason for splitting the steering and speed duties is to avoid distractions by allowing each person to focus on a single task. The Helmsman mistakenly thought the separation of duties was successful and he had control of the ships steering while the Lee Helmsman had full control of the ship's speed. He was partially right. Due to a lack of training, unfamiliarity with the operation of the navigation system, and poor design of the new navigation interface, control was aligned such that the Lee Helmsman had full steering control and control of one of the propellers. In other words, he had half of the speed control. The Helmsman recognized he did not have steering control and announced *loss of steering* to the bridge.

If you don't have steering control, then it's probably a good idea to start slowing down. The Helmsman made an attempt to slow down both propellers. Since he didn't realize he only had control of one propeller, just the port propeller slowed, and the starboard propeller maintained its speed. This caused the McCain to turn sharply into the path of the container ship. Confusion around the operation of the navigation system led to the McCain being uncontrolled for three minutes. The crew realized what had happened and regained control of the destroyer but were unable to get out of the path of the container ship and the two collided moments later.

The impact caused extensive damage to the USS McCain. Ten sailors perished from either being crushed while in their racks or from drowning as their berthing area was flooded. Forty-eight sailors were injured, and the McCain sustained $100 million dollars in damage.

While there were many contributing factors, such as inexperience and fatigue, one of the major NTSB findings was a lack of sufficient training provided to the sailors. The navigation system was recently upgraded to replace the manual controls with electronic controls and this new system was less than a year old. While there was a qualification process in place for these system changes, the NTSB found that the training provided failed to give the crew a good working knowledge of the new controls.

A lack of good training resulted in a significant loss of life, multiple injuries, and substantial financial costs. While training on a new system, process, or job duties may seem fundamental to success, it's often something that gets short-changed. Employees, conditioned to *make it work* almost every day on the job, seldom speak up and admit they are uncomfortable or unsure of what to do. This leaves them to figure out their own version of *what good looks like* for the tasks at hand. When their training is insufficient, workers struggle to fill in the blanks.

Remember the Culture Cycle? When workers haven't been given the knowledge they need, their beliefs are misinformed and incomplete. These beliefs heavily influence their behaviors. If their beliefs or understanding of the situation is off, then it shouldn't come as a surprise when they exhibit the *wrong* behaviors and get results you don't want. They are routinely forced into one of two options: stop and get help (if time allows) or make an educated guess and hope for the best.

You usually don't get too many arguments against the idea of training being good. The debate is usually centered around how much and what kind. When it comes to adopting Human Performance, the options can range from a week-long HP bootcamp to a PowerPoint deck to click through, to a trainer talking about HP at the last safety summit. The typical HP training is an in-person, day long presentation that teaches HP Fundamentals, recognizing Error Traps, mitigating those traps with HP Tools, and a field-guide to help you remember it all. This can be effective if well executed and relatable to the worker. The trick is avoiding some of the pitfalls mentioned earlier, such as trying to cut and paste what other industries do, not giving workers a good vision of how to apply this new HP information to their job, or not continually reinforcing their training. Again, remember the Culture Cycle.

Influencing beliefs is not a one-time training event if you want to permanently shape behaviors.

In its early days, KnowledgeVine took the classroom training approach to helping organizations learn Human Performance; that didn't last long.

First, it was cost prohibitive to many organizations. The expense of paying their people to be in a classroom, coupled with the lost productivity or missed billable work, was too much for many organizations to bear. One client said that the cost of the training itself was only one quarter of the training budget. The rest of the budget was accounted for in employee wages, travel costs, facility expenses, but mostly in lost productivity.

Second, was gaining a better appreciation for how quickly everyone forgets training.

One of our very first clients asked us to go into the field to assess how well their workers were utilizing the HP training we provided. What we found were people struggling to understand what they should do differently, if anything, on the job. One person put it to us this way, "On Thursday my coworkers and I were on the job. On Friday, we went to a conference room and learned about Human Performance. In that conference room, away from the job, it made sense and I could envision how I could apply it to my job. On Monday, we all arrived back at the job, looked at each other and said, 'What do we do now?' We decided to go back to what we were doing on Thursday."

This wasn't out of maliciousness or blatant noncompliance. It's forgetting your training, and instead of struggling through what you could remember, deciding to go back to what you know. This isn't people who just didn't get it or a failure to make the training understandable; it's human nature to forget. The rate at which training is forgotten is pretty staggering.

The Ebbinghaus Forgetting Curve shows how quickly you forget the information presented to you. Ebbinghaus found that you will forget 67% within one day and 79% within three weeks after a one-time class. If you're lucky, the workers remember where they left their field-guides come Monday morning.

It's not that they weren't paying attention or are particularly forgetful. Learning and remembering a new process, especially something that is asking for behavior change and culture shift, can't be accomplished in one training session. The Culture Cycle needs to be influenced continually to produce lasting results. As discussed earlier, if you give HP training to influence the belief that HP is beneficial, the worker may use HP at the next opportunity. However, if the result is exactly the same (with or without HP) then the experience doesn't look any different than what was done on Thursday, right before the HP training. The belief becomes, *If I can get the same result and experience without HP, why bother?*

To ensure we are continually reinforcing the training, and influencing the Culture Cycle, we developed weekly and monthly refreshers or mini training sessions. Of course, we couldn't get our clients' workers into a conference room every week, so these became little training packets delivered via email or through our KnowledgeVine App. The better we got at delivering online training it became apparent that the initial, eight-hour, in classroom training, could be better delivered online as well. This took care of the two problems discussed earlier: cost and information retention.

First, if the training could be presented online, the cost of lost productivity would be minimized. Learners would be able to progress through the training at their own pace. Training could be taken during downtimes. This created significant savings in time and resources.

While it may feel a little unseemly to have the cost as a consideration, the reality is that it always is.

If you have been trying to get your organization onboard with Human Performance for any amount of time, then you know one of the first questions your higher-ups will ask is, "What is this going to cost?" If you can bring HP to them at a lower cost with less lost productivity, then you may be able to move the needle a little easier within your organization.

Second, the information could be spread out and reinforced over time, helping with the rate at which people forget the training. Don't underestimate the difficulty in learning a new process; remember the bad idea of asking your six-year-old to learn how to drive right before heading to Orlando. Sometimes the barrage of information is too much to learn and apply in one sitting. If you can effectively convey the basics, give some guidance for on-the-job usage, and continually reinforce this training, your odds of creating a sustainable solution increase.

Another advantage of online training is accountability. In a classroom setting, it's easy to disengage from the training and not learn anything. Online training generally comes with *knowledge checks* or questions to verify understanding as the training progresses. It's also easy to track who has completed their training and who needs some encouragement or coaching. This is especially important when the sustainability portion of the training is implemented over time as you would want to know who is engaged in their training and who hasn't logged in for months.

A big concern for many organizations is the potential for DRIFT and Human Performance becoming the next in a line of things we used to do. The earlier you can spot drift the better chance you have of turning it around. Online training allows the type of tracking and trending that identifies drift after the first missed training engagement. Usually, drift from standards and expectations tends to creep up on you; only revealed after an accident or injury compels you to take a hard look at your behaviors. Online training can give you real-time insight into the varying levels of engagement within your team.

As stated in an earlier chapter, we are sharing what has worked for KnowledgeVine and the reasons why we have an affinity for a particular process. Some of the lessons were learned the hard way, and we would like others to avoid similar misfires in execution. This isn't to imply that training platforms other than online learning won't work; these are just our preferences for getting over certain hurdles. If online learning isn't appropriate for your organization, then by all means, deploy your

Human Performance training in other ways. Doing something is better than doing nothing, but whatever you do make sure the training is applicable to your people.

Whatever the delivery method, the content needs to be easy to understand. Human Performance technology has been around for decades and there is a wealth of information available. Most training programs fall into the trap of information overload. The more you study Human Performance, the more you find that you like, so it's difficult to exclude any valuable information. This creates a tendency to throw the kitchen sink at your workers since you don't want to deprive them of any good ideas. This kind of training ends up making the same mistake this book is trying to avoid—too many ideas (trees) so you lose your understanding of the high-level goals (forest).

Keep it simple.

Vince Lombardi was well known for starting each new season by holding up a football to his team and saying "Gentlemen, this is a football." He didn't want his team getting too granular before he was sure they understood the larger concepts; and these were professional football players to whom he was talking. Imagine your team, having never heard about Human Performance, now being asked to understand concepts like normalization of deviation, latent organizational weaknesses, or error precursors. It would be like taking a person who had never seen a football game and asking them to run a play called "spider 2-Y banana, 34/35 cowboy, on two." It's simply too much information.

A good example of *too much, too soon* was when KnowledgeVine was asked to help a company reinvigorate their HP process. This organization, we'll call them ABC, had put in a good amount of work to create a robust HP program, and had rolled it out to all their employees the previous year. ABC was now recognizing that HP behaviors were not being exhibited by the workers in the field and were looking for solutions.

With their leadership team, we looked at the company's process to see if we could help them reinvigorate it. The first clue that the problem might be information overload was their human performance field guide. It was over 50 pages long! That's closer to a thesis than a quick reference. Imbedded in the guide were 18 Human Performance Tools and 23 Human Performance Traps. Their initial training was closer to "spider 2 Y banana" than "Gentleman, this is a football." They had overwhelmed their people. Instead of creating a belief that Human Performance is beneficial, the company created an experience that was confusing and stress inducing; and it wasn't just the workers who were unable to absorb all this new information.

In addition to the leadership in the room, the team that created their HP process was there too. When it was pointed out that 18 HP Tools was too much, it was met with a little skepticism. They argued that HP Tools were not hard to understand and should be easy to apply while working in the field. To make the point that they were underestimating the learning curve, they were challenged to list eight HP Tools from memory. They had 18 HP Tools, so it should be easy to list eight of them. As a group, they got to six. These were the people who literally wrote the book, and they couldn't remember their HP training. Of course, the point of a field guide is so workers don't need to memorize everything. But to have a good working knowledge, you should remember enough to be able to apply it as you work. Besides, if you went in the field right now, how many people have their field guide on their person and not buried in a toolbox or desk drawer? On the off chance it occurs to them that NOW might be a good time apply HP to their work, do you think they are going to drop their tools and go get their field guide? Probably not.

Their program wasn't broken, it was just too much for an initial introduction. We advised ABC to not throw out the process they had invested so much energy and effort into but to instead determine the top four most impactful HP Tools and the top four most consequential HP

Traps. Once this group made the determination, they agreed to make these their focus areas. Coach and train on four Tools and four Traps to the point where workers don't need a field guide to remember and apply them. Do this for several months, then introduce other Tools and Traps to expand worker knowledge. This approach was much more successful, and the company began to see HP behaviors exhibited in the field. They didn't need to throw out the work they had done, the company only needed to make its training easier to understand, remember, and apply.

This is the approach that KnowledgeVine takes when introducing Human Performance to an organization. This is why we focus on what we like to call the Core Four Tools and Traps.

HUMAN PERFORMANCE TOOLS

SELF-CHECK
QUESTIONING ATTITUDE
EFFECTIVE COMMUNICATION
PEER-CHECK

HUMAN PERFORMANCE TRAPS

TIME PRESSURE
OVERCONFIDENCE
DISTRACTIONS
VAGUE GUIDANCE

That's it. Four Tools and Four Traps.

Instead of issuing the workers a field guide, we put the more detailed information on an App they can readily access; people will quickly lose their field guides but seldom lose their phones. We also put the simple prompts we need them to remember while working in the field on a wallet sized, plastic card that can hang from a lanyard or attach to a clipboard. There are also magnet and sticker versions of the in-field prompts they can attach to clipboards, toolboxes, or equipment.

Use anything possible to keep HP top of mind, easy to remember, readily available, and convenient to use. The easier you make it, the more you'll get of it.

While there is so much more to learn about Human Performance, let's not take too big of a bite and get overwhelmed. Besides, if your team can get really good at recognizing Time-pressure, Overconfidence, Distractions, and Vague Guidance while mitigating these traps with Self-Checking, Questioning Attitude, Effective Communication, and Peer-Checking, then you are 90% of the way to getting the behaviors you want.

Don't make perfect the enemy of good.

You want to capture that final 10% eventually, but like most processes, that last 10% seems like 50% of your effort. Spread that effort out over time, and don't let it impede the progress you could be making right now. After all, something you can do now is always better than anything that never gets started.

Now that your team has knowledge of Human Performance, you have started to shape their beliefs within the Culture Cycle. But you aren't just looking to impact beliefs. You want those beliefs to shape the behaviors to provide the results you need. How does your team take their knowledge of Human Performance and apply it to their jobs? This is why you need to Apply a strategy for Human Performance within your organization.

CHAPTER 9

APPLY

"We are what we repeatedly do. Excellence, then, is not an act, but a habit."

~ Aristotle (384–322 BC)

You may have heard the story of former neurosurgeon Christopher Duntsch. He first came into national attention in 2018 when his tale was popularized in a podcast titled, *Dr. Death*. It was also made into an NBC mini-series of the same name and has been featured by several other programs on other networks. It's a pretty remarkable story that emphasizes the importance of learning how to take the knowledge out of your head and effectively apply it with your hands.

Christopher Duntsch by all accounts was a successful student. So much so that he was accepted into a particularly challenging MD-PhD program. He completed his neurosurgery residency at the University of Tennessee Health and Science Center and a spine fellowship program at the Semmes-Murphey Clinic in Memphis. Between undergraduate, medical school, residency, and his fellowship, Christopher Duntsch had over 15 years of training.

In his early career he focused on the PhD portion of his training, getting his name on several published papers and patents while also participating in a few biotech startups; utilizing his years of medical training but not applying it to hands-on work. However, the lure of neurosurgery, and its lucrative wages, soon pulled Duntsch to the Dallas, Texas area where he attempted to apply his knowledge as a surgeon within several hospital systems. This was where Christopher Duntsch earned the nickname, *Dr. Death*.

The list of patients who left his surgery table in worse condition than when they arrived is long; some never survived their encounter with Christopher Duntsch at all. At his first hospital, Baylor Plano, many of the other medical professionals raised concerns about his skill as a surgeon after a series of failed surgeries and some disturbing personal behavior. His surgical privileges at Baylor Plano were revoked after one of his patients bled to death from a major arterial injury sustained during one of Duntsch's spinal surgeries.

With his extensive credentials and training, Duntsch was able to get temporary privileges at the nearby Dallas Medical Center, pending a review of his records from his time at Baylor Plano. He lasted less than a week, but in that short time was able to maim one patient and kill another: again, from massive blood loss during his surgery.

After he was dismissed from the Dallas Medical Center, Duntsch was able to obtain surgical privileges at South Hampton Community Hospital and at an outpatient clinic, both in the Dallas area. After several more botched surgeries Duntsch was finally brought before the Texas Medical Board and in 2013 his medical license was revoked due to a "pattern of patient injury."

In 2015, Duntsch was arrested and charged with several felony counts of assault with a deadly weapon causing serious bodily injury. It took a couple of years for his case to go to trial but during the proceedings his defense argued that his actions were well intentioned albeit the result of poor training and a lack of oversight from the hospitals that granted him surgical privileges. In 2017, he was found guilty and sentenced to life in prison. He will be eligible for parole in 2045. He will be 74 years old.

So how was this doctor, with over 15 years of training, so bad at his job? How was he not able to take his extensive medical knowledge and apply it successfully to his work? One reason is the fact that he received very little hands-on training to learn how to apply the knowledge he gained in the classroom.

The progression through the medical profession is not unlike any other apprenticeship training. Whether you're going to be a plant operator or get a commercial driver's license, step number one is always classroom training to learn the basics before you are allowed to put your hands on plant equipment or get into the driver's seat of a tractor-trailer. Of course, medical students have several years of academic learning before they start working on actual patients. After a couple of years in the classroom, medical students will then work different clinical rotations to gain a deeper understanding of the various fields of medicine. While they are working around patients, this should not be considered *extensive hands-on training*. Students can perform some minor procedures, under supervision, but while they are still medical students, their day mostly involves getting quizzed by more senior medical professionals to assess their knowledge and potential fit in the medical field. The vast majority of their *hands-on* training comes after they graduate medical school and are accepted into a residency program to be trained in their specific field of medicine. This is like obtaining a CDL learner's permit and now you can drive with an instructor or stand *under instruction* watches in the plant with a qualified operator. This is where you now apply theory to practice under the watchful eye of a knowledgeable leader.

As you can imagine, a doctor's hands-on, residency program can last anywhere from three to ten years depending on the complexity of the field of study. This is typically followed with more training in a fellowship program where doctors get even more specific training. Again, think of it like the CDL driver. It's one thing to be qualified to drive a tractor-trailer but if you want to haul hazardous chemicals, then you'll need some more specific training. Given the complexities of the human body and delicate nature of surgery, most doctors completing their surgical residency training will participate in over 1,000 surgeries as part of their hands-on education. Christopher Duntsch participated in fewer than one hundred. He was somehow able to slip through the cracks and completed his surgical residency with shockingly little hands-on training.

Despite his 15 years of medical training, Christopher Duntsch managed to avoid getting the training he needed to apply his medical knowledge to the actual work of spinal surgery; and it showed. There's little doubt that he had the knowledge, but he didn't have the practical skills. While this is an extreme example of an inability to apply information to a job, rolling out Human Performance training without a plan for teaching people how to apply it, is just as foolhardy as not sending surgeons through residency, letting operators put their hands on the plant after passing a test, or letting commercial truck drivers have free reign of the highways with only a learner's permit.

It's not enough to know WHAT to do.

You must have a plan to teach your workers how to make practical use of this knowledge and apply it to their jobs. Broadly, this plan needs to include two things:

- Clear, observable actions the individual should take

- Coaching to refine the behaviors you see

Clear actions aren't just ideas like "be safe" or even guidance to "look for HP traps." There needs to be concrete standards for what *good looks like* within your organization that are observable and assessable.

This can be accomplished in several ways. Instead of saying, "Use HP on the job," there needs to be clear expectations set for how Human Performance is applied to the job.

For example:

- It is now a requirement that HP Traps are identified on every pre-job brief and mitigating steps are also documented. To help with this, we have changed the pre-job form to include these items.

- Procedures have been revised to identify critical steps where Self-Checking or Peer-Checking should be used. It is a requirement that workers pause at these steps and obtain a Peer-check to assess if conditions are safe to proceed.

- Post job reviews are required to be conducted and documented. Near misses and areas for improvement must be included.

- When communicating critical data, such as measurements, gauge readings, system parameters, or giving directions, three-part communication, the phonetic alphabet, and single digits, must be used to avoid confusion or miscommunication.

- After arriving at the job site, but before commencing work, all workers must pause to assess the work environment, consider HP Traps and Tools, and to ensure unexpected hazards are not present.

The list can go on, but each of these examples are observable and assessable. How easy is it to watch a pre-job brief or JOB SAFETY ANALYSIS (JSA) to see if HP was discussed, to notice if workers paused at a critical step, or completed a post job review? It's pretty obvious when someone says *A* instead of *Alpha* or doesn't repeat back directions. How easy is it to see if the crew takes a moment to assess the worksite rather than just getting after it? The workers are clear about what they need to do and it's easy for supervisors to see if it was done. The supervisor doesn't need to look at their workers and wonder, "Are they using a Questioning Attitude?" You can see by their actions that they are following the expectations to use Human Performance in their work. This makes coaching easier for the supervisor, who is likely new to HP themselves.

Back to the Culture Cycle. Workers are given the information they need in their initial training. If well presented (And why wouldn't it be? You read the previous chapter and avoided all the pitfalls.), then this new information will influence their beliefs. If they believe HP is good for them and they also believe they will be accountable for using HP, then there should be different behaviors exhibited. When your coaches are in the field reinforcing these clear and observable expectations, and engaging the workers about them, this will impact their behaviors as well, if for no other reason than they are being watched and have set observable expectations.

In any event, you want to avoid the HP Trap of Vague Guidance when setting expectations for the use of HP. Issuing directives like, "Use HP on the job" or "Look for HP Traps" is too vague to be enforceable or even coachable. A supervisor who is new to Human Performance would likely have a difficult time defining what it looks like when a member of their team is Self-Checking or using a Questioning Attitude. If you can't see it, how do you know if they are doing it? And if you don't know they are doing it, how can you coach it? If you can't see it and assess it, then how do you measure progress?

Think about a newly licensed, teenage driver. They passed a written test demonstrating they know the basic rules of driving. They spent some time learning from a qualified instructor to learn how to apply this knowledge to the act of driving. After a while, they passed a *hands-on driving-skills assessment* from the state and are now licensed to drive. If all the coaching they received from that point forward was a vague, "Be safe" before they get on the road, then there isn't really any coaching happening at all.

What does *be safe* mean to a young driver? They are left to fill in the blanks with whatever *safe* means to them, and their vision of safety may not align with yours. If you're not actively coaching on behaviors, there's a good chance that *hands at ten and two* has devolved into one hand on the wheel and the cell phone that used to be in the center console is now in their other hand. After an accident or ticket, you can probably pinpoint the unsafe behaviors that preceded it, but what could have been discussed if you were engaged in coaching? You can argue if the driver is *being safe* but it's hard to argue more specific standards like stay under the speed limit, stay three seconds back, or use your turn signals to be predictable to others; you either are or you aren't and there's no guesswork or debate.

Similarly, when setting expectations ensure they are specific and observable so they can be coached. Don't just ask for vague behaviors like *Use Human Performance* or even *Stop when unsure*. Let them know a specific behavior you want to see when using Human Performance:

- When you Self-Check, I want to see you physically stop and consider your next steps before taking action.

- When you use Effective Communication to relay critical information or instructions, I want to hear three-part communication, phonetic letters, and single digits to avoid miscommunications.

- I want to see you Self-Checking by comparing equipment labels and tags against switching orders, procedures, lock-out/tag-out instructions, or other written guidance. Touch and verify the label before manipulating equipment.

- To know you are using a Questioning Attitude, I need to hear you challenge vague words like probably, mostly, should, I think, usually, etc.

- When using a Peer-Check, I need to hear both people verbalizing their next step, this way both workers are predictable in their actions.

- I want to see clear agreement before action is taken when Peer-Checking. I need to hear constant chatter between the two workers to ensure they are on the same page.

Remember the guidance suggested earlier for the effective application of the Human Performance information they received in their training: give your people clear, observable actions to take so your coaches have an easier time assessing these actions and coaching them when necessary.

Give them tools and job aids that you can see them use. Refine processes, change procedures, amend paperwork, and improve how work is done to incorporate use of these new HP behaviors.

Don't roll out changes to how your team approaches and performs work and expect it to be executed flawlessly.

Be prepared to help them apply this new Human Performance knowledge, because knowledge by itself doesn't improve safety; the behaviors this knowledge promotes are what actually move the needle.

CHAPTER 10

SUSTAIN

"Investing in the safety and health of workers is about growing a culture; not simply developing a safety management program and then hoping it works- you have to feed it and care for it so that it succeeds and continues to succeed."

~ David Michaels, PhD MPH

What do Myanmar, Liberia, and United States of America all have in common? These are the three countries in the world still widely using the Imperial System for its units of measurement. With the US's influence on global trade, other countries will recognize elements of the Imperial System, but the Metric System is their official units of measurement and the system most commonly used in their everyday lives. Likewise, Myanmar, Liberia, and United States will recognize and utilize elements of the metric system, like that two liter of Coke (soda) or that kilo of coke (not soda). However, the most widely used system, day-to-day, in these three countries, remains the Imperial. The United States may soon find itself all alone in its use of inches, ounces, miles, and gallons since Myanmar and Liberia have started to move their countries to the Metric System. [9]

It's not like the United States has never seen the value of a globally unified system of measurement. In fact, the US was one of the original signors of the Treaty of the Meter back in 1877. This treaty refined and established the Metric System as the official unit of measure for worldwide use. The US officially had a clear preference for the Metric System but did not have a plan for implementing this change. As you no doubt have recognized, had the US implemented this change with **DIAS** (Discover, Inform, Apply, and Sustain), Americans would all be complaining about high gas prices in terms of kilometers per liter. But by all accounts, the only thing that happened was an attempt to inform Americans about the Metric System: "Here's a system related to your current way of doing business that we think is better. Enjoy!"

Just like rolling out Human Performance on Friday with no other strategy, guess what the average American did on Monday? Yep. They looked at the Metric System and said, "That makes sense but I'm going back to what I did on Thursday because it's familiar and still works."

Despite America's lack of change management, the metric system never completely went away. Americans just memorized ratios for when accurately converting Metric to Imperial was crucial or were OK with *a meter is about a yard* when estimating was good enough. This went on until the early 1960s, when the United Kingdom started to transition their country to the Metric System to better trade with their European counterparts. This spurred the United States to take another look at moving to the Metric System.

In 1968, the US Congress authorized a three-year study to assess the feasibility of the United States adopting metric units; now called International Standard (SI) measurements. The final report titled, "A Metric America: A Decision Whose Time Has Come," not only spoiled the ending for the avid congressional report reader, but, now unsurprisingly, advocated for the United States to transition to the SI system. This report recommended to Congress a 10-year implementation plan to carefully transition the United States away from the Imperial System.

Based on the recommendation of this report, the US Congress passed the Metric Conversion Act of 1975 to facilitate the use of the International Standard system in America. The Act established the US Metric Board whose job it was to guide the American people through this change. This board was tasked with helping the States and businesses apply the change to metric units to their work. Each State was given a set of calibrated metric standards and educational resources were made available.

This plan has more elements of DIAS than the previous attempt at converting the US to Metric.

DISCOVER: The US Congress actually put together a 45-member advisory panel to study the feasibility of a metric conversion. This panel returned the 191-page report, "A Metric America: A Decision Whose Time Has Come." Not a bad attempt at discovery and planning.

INFORM: The Metric Conversion Act of 1975 established the US Metric Board, tasked with providing educational resources to States and businesses as they make the transition.

APPLY: The US Metric Board also provided support and guidance to help States and private businesses in their adoption of International Standards, kind of like coaching. Each State was even given job aids in the form of official, calibrated metric standards for them to reference and use.

SUSTAIN: This is where it all falls apart and why Americans still have foot-long hotdogs.

The one thing the Metric Conversion Act of 1975 did not do was to implement the 10-year conversion plan the panel recommended. The panel recognized the need to sustain change over time so it will stick, but Congress didn't make that a priority. To make matters worse, Congress decided that adopting the International Standards system should be completely voluntary.

Without any real plan to sustain the momentum and no motivation for States, businesses, and individuals to change, the push for the International Standards system never gained any traction. By 1982, with no significant progress having been made in the metrification of the United States, the Reagan administration abolished the Metric Board, effectively ending the push for the International Standards system.

Today, the Metric system is still the officially preferred system of weights and measures in the United States. However, the Imperial

System standards are the units of measure widely used by the majority of US citizens. Remember how we defined organizational culture? It's not the stated mission, vision, and values of the organization. It's the sum of all the actions of individual members of the organization. The US government tried to shape and define the culture by saying, "We are a Metric country." However, the day-to-day actions of US citizens indicates the *actual* culture is far from what the government *wanted*.

The failure of the US government to move the population to the International Standards system can be traced to two missteps:

- They studied, planned, educated, and offered assistance but didn't implement the long-term plan to sustain any momentum they gained from these efforts.

- The program lacked any accountability, so individuals and businesses just waited them out until the current culture prevailed.

If your organization has tried and failed in any change efforts, there's a good chance that you could trace the lack of success to not having a long-term plan to sustain momentum and/or a lack of accountability for anyone to follow the lead.

*Culture is strong and will fight you;
and 75% of the time it will win.*

The current culture of your organization was built over years, and it will take time to reshape and transform it. Don't underestimate how long it takes to shape something as powerful and slow moving as your organization's culture. You certainly don't want to put effort into discovering the current culture, organizing training to inform your team about Human Performance basics, and coaching your team on how to apply this new information to their specific jobs, only to watch the culture drift back into old habits. Sustain the momentum and drive accountability to have an evolving Human Performance culture.

Accountability has been woven throughout the KnowledgeVine process. As you recall, it started with our first interaction with the client's workforce during the Discover phase—the Culture Survey. While the survey is anonymous, it is our first indication of how closely the employees follow the expectations of their leadership. During the Inform phase, individual workers are tracked and held accountable within the learning management system. As we touched on in the Inform chapter, in addition to its convenience, accessibility, efficiency, and effectiveness, online learning has the additional benefit of tracking individual engagement, or lack of it. During the Apply phase, we ensured the expectations set were observable and measurable. This also helps to drive accountability when your leaders can easily and clearly assess who is demonstrating the desired behaviors. When you can see who is rowing and who is simply along for the ride, you can better target accountability.

While accountability has been part of the fabric of REMEDY and DIAS, there is no greater need for it than during the Sustain phase. This is when the newness has started to wear off and the organization has started to drift back to old cultural norms. This is the time to keep the information flowing to your team and to have a lens into the amount of drift you are experiencing.

When we previously discussed the Culture Cycle, we pointed out that the cycle is not a one-and-done process. There needs to be constant influence on the Culture Cycle to create the results you want. Over time, the new beliefs, behaviors, results, and experiences of each individual will feed into and inform the larger culture of the organization; but it takes time and attention. This is why, at KnowledgeVine, the Sustain portion of DIAS takes the longest amount of time and doesn't get shortchanged.

The entire DIAS process is 24 months:

DISCOVER: Organizations usually take about one to two months to complete the Culture Survey.

INFORM: While the training is only about two hours long, it is presented over several online modules. Individuals are given two months to complete this initial training.

APPLY: Once the initial training is completed, the in-field application training starts. This should be an ongoing process, but we understand that leaders are also susceptible to drifting and run the risk of slowing or stopping coaching. This is why Sustain runs simultaneously with Apply.

SUSTAIN: Occurs over the remaining 18-20 months.

As you can see, the bulk of the time is spent on sustaining the momentum created by the first three phases. The good news is that it also requires the least amount of effort. The training conducted during Inform is new and detailed. The behaviors we ask each person to Apply to their work is unfamiliar and possibly uncomfortable. While the time spent in Inform and Apply is much shorter, it's also the time where most of the heavy lifting is done. Sustain is simply reinforcing the work previously accomplished.

Think of this change like correcting course and safely navigating a barge on the river. If you needed to get the barge off the bank, into the river channel, and moving safely down the river, the vast majority of your effort would be in getting the barge unstuck and turned in the right direction. Once you're in the river channel, steering the barge is easy. However, if you take your hands off the wheel, you're likely to drift right back into the riverbank. Navigating the barge in the channel is LOW effort but is also CONSTANT effort. Don't take your hands off the wheel once you are in safe waters.

To maintain momentum, drive accountability, and keep Human Performance *top of mind*, KnowledgeVine continues engagement by keeping a trickle-feed of information to the organization. Again, utilizing the convenience and efficiency of digital platforms, each leader will be given three-to-five-minute packets of training every week or two to share with their workgroups. These are usually presented in the form of a mini-online training, video clip, audio file, or informative flyer to review. The training will cover a wide range of Human Performance topics and serve as a refresher for the information already learned but has likely been forgotten. (Remember the forgetting curve?) This sustainability content is often used as safety topics or as prompts for group discussions pertaining to Human Performance within work groups.

Since this content is delivered through an online learning management system (LMS) staff are already a part of this provides the added benefit of spotting drift more quickly than previously available. Once the user consumes sustainability content, the LMS system gives them credit for completing this short course. After the first missed engagement, leaders and executives can know if someone is starting to drift away from the Human Performance process. This allows the leader to quickly provide coaching to help them get back on track. This is influencing the Culture Cycle early and often and before old habits creep back in; navigating the barge with small and timely adjustments to avoid the dreaded banks.

There's also a secondary benefit on the Culture Cycle— encouraging participation. As previously discussed, many workers will simply *wait it out* to see if this new Human Performance thing *is here to stay and worth their effort*. The first sign that HP may not stick around long term is a lack of visibility after the initial training. We start out hot, but after an initial surge of information (and hopefully some coaching) there is a noticeable fall in effort from the organization. With Sustain, each packet of information about a Human Performance concept also serves as a reminder that the organization is still serious about HP and waiting it out is not an option. It'll take longer for some than others to understand your HP efforts are not a flavor of the month idea, or the latest in a line of failed initiatives, but eventually everyone gets the message; and 24 months is more than long enough to get the last of the holdouts off the sidelines.

While you may not have the option of a learning management system, you still must create a strategy to sustain the momentum towards a Human Performance culture. Find ways to keep a trickle of information flowing to your team with handouts or job aids. Incorporate Human Performance into your communications. Badging items like posters, stickers, magnets, and banners are not a fix-all but can have an important role. While they can soon become background noise, the fact that the organization took the time and effort to provide them signals to workers that this is not a temporary process. Ensure your safety moments include a discussion about what HP Trap was present and which HP Tool could have mitigated it. When coaching is done in the field, ensure it involves a discussion about Human Performance.

It takes great planning, effort, and resources to start creating a Human Performance culture, but all it takes for it to fail is to do nothing after the initial surge of training is over. Keeping the momentum going is the difference between, "We have a Human Performance culture," and "We tried to adopt Human Performance once." Inch by inch (centimeter by centimeter), your plan to sustain momentum will move your team closer to a Human Performance culture. Soon enough you'll find yourselves miles (kilometers) ahead of where you were as an organization and without an ounce (gram) of regret for the effort.

CHAPTER 11

PART I WRAP-UP
THE FOREST

*Mr. Jowett, of Birmingham, tells of a lay preachers'
conference, in which a veteran described his method of
sermon preparation.
"I take my text," he said, "and divide my sermon into
three parts. In the first part I tell 'em what I am going to
tell 'em; in the second part—well, I tell 'em; in the third
part, I tell 'em what I've told 'em."*

~ The "Sunday Strand"

As you may have guessed, we shared what would be presented in
the introduction, followed by several chapters delivering this
information, and now we are wrapping up Part I where we will quickly
look back on what has been covered. By way of review, let's look at what
we promised to tell you in the introduction:

- Know what you're up against by understanding the strength
  and importance of organizational culture—**Chapter 1.**

- Look at how individuals are simultaneously creating the
  culture while also being influenced by it (The Culture
  Cycle)—**Chapter 1.**

- Learn the broad strategy for creating a Human Performance
  culture (REMEDY formula)—**Chapter 2.**

- Understand how each level of the organization can start
  working together toward the common goal of creating a
  Human Performance culture (REMEDY Matrix)—**Chapter 3.**

- Determine WHY we get certain behaviors to target our
  corrective actions (WHY)—**Chapters 4 and 5.**

- Develop a change management strategy with Human Performance in mind (DIAS)—**Chapters 6 through 10.**

Don't lose sight of the forest...

Your culture has been created over time and has deep roots in your organization. Any efforts to evolve your culture will take time and a good plan; there are no shortcuts. The sum of all your individual behaviors is what defines your organizational culture. The Culture Cycle helps you understand how to influence individual behaviors and informs your strategy to ensure your efforts are targeted in the right areas. The REMEDY formula is a broad HP strategy that addresses the need to manage culture change. Organizational change is not one-size-fits-all; just as in your normal work, different levels of the organization have different roles and responsibilities.

The REMEDY Matrix defines these various roles and responsibilities across three levels of the organization: Executives, Leaders, and Employees. Understand why you are getting specific behaviors and how knowing this can help you to find better solutions.

With this broad strategy in mind, there needs to be solid tactics for implementing this strategy. This is where DIAS can help. You need to DISCOVER where you are as an organization to best understand the path forward and the challenges ahead. You must effectively INFORM your team about the fundamentals of Human Performance, so they have a clear vision of what is expected. Your team needs to be coached on how to APPLY this vision to their actual work. To prevent the old culture from re-emerging, your team needs to be accountable and consistently engaged in Human Performance through a constant flow of information and coaching to help them SUSTAIN your hard-earned momentum.

While never losing sight of the forest, it's time to get more granular and take a closer look at the trees: the specifics of each section of the REMEDY Matrix.

To this point, we have explored the idea that each person has a different role within the organization. For example, starting in the top-left of the REMEDY Matrix, Executives have the responsibility to Set Expectations for the use of Human Performance within their organization. While this starts to bring into focus the role of the Executive in creating a Human Performance culture, there is still much more to understand in order to take effective action. There are still questions around what it means to Set Expectations. Why is it important? How do I do it? How does this relate to the Culture Survey results? How do the behaviors we see tell us if we are working in the right areas? What are some tips, tricks, and lessons learned?

The answers to these questions are found in Part II—The Trees. Each chapter in Part II will go into greater detail regarding a specific block of the REMEDY Matrix. It's full of useful information that you can apply to your current work, but it's also easy to lose sight of why you do it.

Remember: these specific actions are intended to influence the Culture Cycle toward evolving a Human Performance culture.

Keep this in mind as you learn more about the specific actions you can take every day to drive continuous improvement in your organization.

REMEDY®

PART II
THE TREES
SPECIFIC ACTIONS

REMEDY®

SPECIFIC ACTIONS

You cannot hope to build a better world without improving the individuals. To that end, each of us must work for his own improvement and, at the same time, share a general responsibility for all humanity, our particular duty being to aid those to whom we think we can be most useful.

~ Marie Curie (1867 – 1934)

Roles and responsibilities vary for each person in the organization. The workers in the boardroom do not have the same day-to-day responsibilities as the workers in the toolroom. Remember the example of the football team to illustrate the typical organizational hierarchy?

OWNERS AND GENERAL MANAGERS

COACHES AND TRAINERS

PLAYERS AND SUPPORT STAFF

Everyone has the same organizational goal, but each person has their own unique role in helping the team accomplish this goal, which in this case, is winning games.

Similarly, your team can be divided into three broad areas:

EXECUTIVES

LEADERS

EMPLOYEES

Each person in your organization shares the goal of creating a Human Performance culture but everyone will have different roles and responsibilities in helping the team accomplish this. As you recall, this is the reason for the REMEDY Matrix; helping each person in the organization to understand their unique role in implementing and sustaining a Human Performance culture.

The REMEDY Matrix has, thus far, been presented in broad terms. As you can imagine, there is a great deal of information behind each block of the Matrix. Let's start by better understanding the roles and influences of each level in your organization. These are the roles found in the horizontal columns of the following image, representing the REMEDY Matrix.

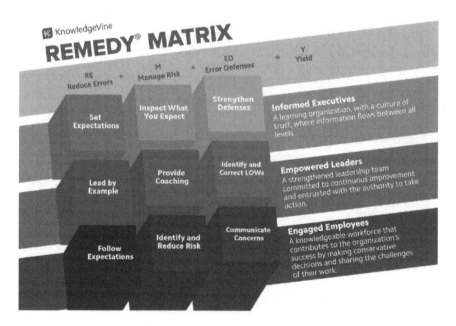

INFORMED EXECUTIVES

The first level in a healthy, effective organization is that of INFORMED EXECUTIVES who encourage a culture of trust which allows information to flow between all levels. The extent to which Executives are aware of organizational performance and the things that may be hindering it, the more likely the organization will have a healthy, vibrant culture. The goal of the REMEDY Matrix is to create better informed upper leadership, hence the name, Informed Executives.

Most Executives will readily admit that there is a lack of information flowing between the layers of their organization. This is often called a *clay layer* in reference to the layer of earth which will impede the flow of water. It's important to permeate this organizational clay layer for the Executive level to better understand the challenges their workforce is facing. Workers often know what is broken and have good insight into a solution. Executives have the authority to fix what is broken, but often don't have the information they need to make the best decisions.

One thing that prevents the sharing of information is a lack of trust. Employees want to see that the actions of the senior leaders are aligned with WHAT they say, because that establishes what it's like to work at your company and builds a level of trust. Executives set broad organizational goals and guide the direction of the team. While they may not be engaged in the details of how work is accomplished, they certainly have a significant influence on it. HOW they wield this influence is always under scrutiny. How do you think it impacts the workers when you talk about how important it is to be on time, but you are routinely late for meetings? Or, if you talk about how much value you place on family time, but you often work late into the evening and call your employees in on the weekends without blinking an eye. Or worse yet, you ask for near-miss reporting but then you discipline someone for a near-miss.

Workers will never trust you if they don't believe you, and if they don't trust you, they will only tell you the things they think you want to hear. That's not being informed; it's being pacified.

EMPOWERED LEADERS

Leaders in middle-management or front-line leadership roles are in a difficult spot because they get little credit when things go right, and almost all the blame when they don't. A recent survey by CareerBuilder found that more than one-quarter of managers were not ready when they became a leader and 58% said they didn't receive any management training before their promotion. Many of these leaders received a *battlefield promotion* without any development time or training, so they are forced to learn the new role without the benefit of a mentor to guide them through the rough spots. Accordingly, many are promoted because they were the best at their technical job, so the assumption is they will be very good at leading a group of people who do that same job. Technical skills and managerial skills are two vastly different talents.

Some leaders are great coaches and have the skills necessary to manage their work groups. However, these coaches will often get caught up in administrative tasks and don't have the time to utilize their leadership skills.

These same leaders may find it hard to be effective, because while they have the responsibility for safe and efficient work, they do not control all of the necessary resources to do it properly. Typically, concerns should be resolved by the leader that is closest to the worker. They should have the authority to address most issues; with some restrictions of course, such as monetary limitations or not implementing system-wide changes without larger discussions.

When applying Human Performance to this level of leadership, it is crucial to keep in mind that they are caught in the middle. They are the only level in the matrix that needs to strengthen relationships to encourage worker feedback and be entrusted with the authority to act upon it. This is why this group is called the EMPOWERED LEADERS. The goal is to empower a person with the skills they need to manage people and to also empower them with the authority to fix the issues that are within their control.

ENGAGED EMPLOYEES

A 2022 Gallup survey found that 77% of employees are not engaged in what the company is trying to do, and that nearly 6 out of 10 are "quiet quitting," or psychologically disengaged from the work.[10]

These are shocking numbers that tell you the management style that worked in the past is outdated and will only lead you to failure if you perpetuate it. The team dynamics are different and a directive style that doesn't make workers feel included will not work.

This lack of engagement can come from many places. As mentioned earlier, the employee is closest to the problem and likely has the best solution. They have the knowledge but don't have the authority to fix it. They will try a few times to offer solutions but if they see no impact then it's no longer worth the effort to try.

This is the beginning of the clay layer. Information is not being shared because information is not being acted upon.

Employees may also be disengaged because there is a lack of trust in their abilities, or they are looked at as a *necessary evil* to get the work done. Many organizations will lament the amount of turnover but never consider that they are treating their employees like hired guns, easily replaceable and not a critical part of the team. The truth is, if you don't engage your employees, they will leave your company and go somewhere else where these techniques are practiced and go where their efforts are appreciated. Or worse, they will remain disengaged and uninterested in helping your team to improve.

Leaders will not raise the employee engagement numbers by talking about it—they will only raise these numbers through their actions, which likely means changing the culture and the way your senior leaders think. Of course, there are limits to what you can accept—employees can't spend time on social media rather than doing the work you are paying them to do. But rather than complain about the use of new technology, embrace it so you can meet your employees where they are and get your message to them in a way that they are more likely to receive it.

ENGAGED EMPLOYEES, who contribute their experiences, skills, and abilities, help the organization succeed. They will tell you what is broken. They will tell you what makes it difficult to perform their jobs as expected. They will tell you how to improve. Creating Engaged Employees is the goal of the REMEDY Matrix and Human Performance more broadly.

It's not about fixing the worker. It's about engaging the worker to help you fix the culture.

The description of these three levels of the organization forms the deliverable, the Yield. You know you have a healthy and effective organizational culture when you have Informed Executives, Empowered Leaders, and Engaged Employees.

These horizontal rows in the REMEDY Matrix all work toward this common goal: building a Human Performance culture. Human Performance is defined within the elements of the REMEDY Formula:

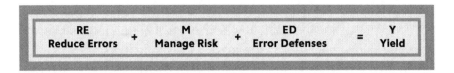

RE		M		ED		Y
Reduce Errors	+	Manage Risk	+	Error Defenses	=	Yield

The REMEDY Formula describes WHAT you need to do, and the REMEDY Matrix defines WHO needs to do each part. As described above, the horizontal rows of the REMEDY Matrix lay out WHO; Informed Executives, Empowered Leaders, and Engaged Employees. Additionally, the vertical columns of the REMEDY Matrix indicated the area of the REMEDY Formula being addressed. In other words, Executives, Leaders, and Employees share the goal of reducing errors and they each have a unique role in accomplishing this.

REDUCE ERRORS

This is an easy place to start, and in the early days of Human Performance, was the only thing you focused on. The REMEDY Matrix addresses overall performance with specific emphasis on each level of the organization, but reducing errors is still the starting point. Mistakes are costly, both in terms of employee health and safety, and the impact on the business. If someone is injured, you will have to provide a prompt explanation for why the event happened. Similarly, if a mistake is made that has a big impact on financial performance, you will be called upon to explain that as well. In either case, your team will likely conclude the event was totally avoidable, but as they develop a corrective action plan will they take actions that preclude this event from happening again? You need to balance the realization that humans are prone to error, with a strategy that reduces the frequency and severity of the mistakes they make.

Manage Risk

Many books have been written on the management of risk and how to address change in an organization, but rarely do you see these principles applied to adopting Human Performance. You draw a line in your mind to define the point at which you will need a formal plan and anything below that line is in the space of "I'll figure it out as I go." This is a response to your determination of risk—if you're leading a big project that simply cannot fail, it's likely you'll have a plan in place to make sure you cover all the bases. The truth is, once you get into this big project and settle into your comfort zone, you go below the line again and there is a tendency to ditch the plan. When given the option to follow a rigorous plan, or adjust in the moment, you ultimately base this decision on your perception of the risk involved and what is easier for you to accomplish. Each level of the organization must understand their role with respect to managing risk; the role of the Engaged Employee to *Identify and Reduce Risk* is much more focused than that of the Informed Executive or the Empowered Leader, but each is important if you want to see success in the end.

Error Defenses

One of the **FIVE PRINCIPLES OF HUMAN** Performance states that system failures contribute to 90% of all errors. When an error occurs, and the first question asked is, "who did it," there is a demonstration of a lack of awareness of this principle. A better question to ask is, "How did this happen?" Error defenses are the processes and systems put in place to diminish the impact of human errors, which can be minimized but can't be eliminated (another of the five Human Performance principles). Examples include policies and procedures, training, signs and postings, corrective action programs, and close call reporting.

If an employee makes an error, it may be that they didn't have enough training, or it may be that the training they had was not accurate. Maybe they followed the procedure step-by-step, but the procedure was wrong, and the error was not their fault. It could be that a similar event happened a few months ago but the issue was not corrected—the can was kicked down the road, setting a trap that resulted in the recent error. Latent Organizational Weaknesses (LOWs) are system breakdowns, or workarounds, which are a set up for failure.

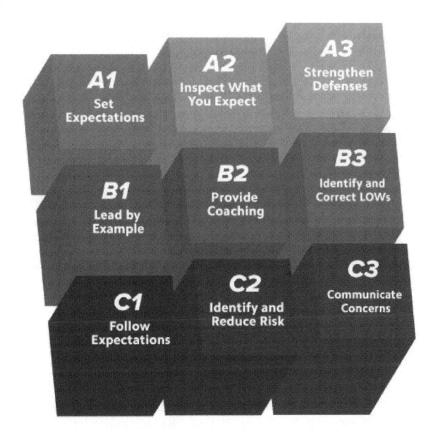

The simplicity of the REMEDY Matrix is that it has something for everyone. The organization is represented by three different levels, and each level has a specific job to improve performance. Again, consider the football team—the Owners are not working to improve their football skills. The Coaches are not negotiating contracts. The players are not concerned with stadium taxes. The Players are training to be the best at their particular role on the team. The absence of this level of focus has been the cause of many organizational failures. As you've learned, when a change initiative is launched without a compelling and agreed-upon reason, you are fighting an uphill battle. Subsequently, if the typical employee question, "What am I expected to do?" is not answered, the organization will not succeed; and workers will go back to what they used to do.

Knowing there is an organizational gap in a particular area of the REMEDY Matrix is great, but what are you going to do about it? As mentioned in Part I, the expectations set by the organization need to be actionable and observable. The actions being offered in Part II will follow these same guidelines. While Part I may have left you with some *Big Ideas*, Part II will offer specific, observable, and measurable actions you can take to address any deficiencies found in a particular area of the REMEDY Matrix.

These actions should be taken at the precursor level; before an accident or injury but after you have identified risky behaviors not aligned with your standards. For this reason, we call them Proactions or actions that proactively eliminate risk BEFORE there is an accident or injury. While these specific actions can be taken AFTER an unwanted event, proactions (yes, it's a word) are most effective when they are used at the precursor level to address an organizational or individual weakness in the REMEDY Matrix. This in turn will help you to close the gap between your standards and behaviors. As you know, when your standards and behaviors are misaligned, you have risk. When you can more closely align your standards and behaviors, you can eliminate risk. See how it's all coming together to influence the Culture Cycle?

- Set clear and effective standards with Human Performance.
- Educate and coach on these standards.
- Find the gaps between behaviors and standards where your risk exists.
- Understand why this risk has occurred to better target your proactions.

- Use proactions to strengthen the standards or coach on behaviors to close this risk gap.

Now you are not only finding gaps, but you are also closing gaps to prevent recurrence. While this is a great strategy, the devil is always in the details.

The following chapters provide actionable details on each of the nine boxes in the REMEDY Matrix and follow this standard pattern:

- Identify the area of the REMEDY Matrix.
- Defining "what good looks like."
- WHY is this role important?
- How to ensure success.
- Understanding how a failure in this area the root cause for could be WHY an undesired behavior has occurred.
- Offer examples of Proactions to address a deficiency.
- How the Culture Survey questions can help you measure success (a detailed response to each of the four survey questions).

This book is different than others. Most books leave you with some good ideas, but great books leave you with a lot to think about. *REMEDY* is intended to present these ideas but to also give you something to do about it. Part II helps you to identify where there is risk and why it is occurring. After completing this book, you can use Part II as a reference to help you take targeted actions to help eliminate this risk and get your behaviors more in line with your standards.

Now let's learn a little more about *what good looks like* and the actions you can take to get there.

REMEDY

INFORMED EXECUTIVES

A1	A2	A3
Set Expectations	Inspect What You Expect	Strengthen Defenses

A1: SET EXPECTATIONS

FORMULA: Reduce Errors

MATRIX: Informed Executives

WHY THE BEHAVIOR OCCURRED: Didn't Know I Should

Defining "Set Expectations"

The organization has created a mission, vision, goals, and values that are communicated and supported. Policies, procedures, and guidelines contribute to error-free performance. The organization implements best practices for error reduction.

Why It's Important

Executives are in a unique position to establish the guiding documents for all employees. This guidance sets the tone and describes the desired culture for the organization, and as such, should be effectively communicated to all employees on a recurring basis. Ideally this will be accomplished through a variety of means as some employees will be more likely to receive the message in writing, while others will prefer something more visual. New employees should be introduced to the company's expectations in orientation. As they gain experience with the team, they should see periodic messages from executives that confirm and reinforce the expectations set by the organization. This process strengthens employee understanding of the expectations and thereby builds on the culture this guidance intends to establish. As simple as this may seem, it is much harder to accomplish in the real world. A recent study found that only 7% of employees today fully understand their company's business strategies and what's expected of them in order to help achieve company goals.[11]

How To Do It

The guidance established by executives is delivered through several means. Most organizations use mission, vision, goals, and values to establish guidance. It's important to understand how these relate to each other. A good analogy is a road trip.

MISSION: Your mission is where you want to go as an organization. The mission of the company communicates the grounding principle for which the organization exists. The mission will serve to remind the team of their purpose, so proper decisions can be made. When decisions are made in alignment with the mission, the organization is on a steady path.

VISION: The company vision defines the extent to which the company can dream and create. While the mission of the company sets the boundaries for operation (what path we will take) the vision allows the team to look ahead and determine the direction down the road.

GOALS: Goals are established as milestones along the path to the company's mission, like mile markers tracking our progress. By setting goals that are in alignment with the mission, the company can measure progress and make necessary adjustments.

VALUES: The company's values describe the traits and culture. Standard values often include safety, character, integrity, and trust. But what about customer service, on-time delivery, or innovation? Are these fundamental values of the organization? While two companies may have the *same mission,* they will often have *a different feel* because of the values within the culture. For example, two companies can move down the same road, toward the same goal, but one chooses to use an EV while the other a horse and buggy.

Executives promote error-free performance by establishing written guidance that directs the work activities of the employees. Policies are issued to set the overall expectations regarding a particular topic; there may be a policy regarding employee vacation or use of company vehicles. Procedures are established to direct specific steps in the conduct of work activities, for example, starting up a system, conducting a quarterly inventory, or obtaining a chemical sample. Procedures provide guidance that ensure consistent, predictable completion of a task by anyone with the requisite training. Guidelines are less formal than a procedure, basically describing the expectations for a task. There may be a guideline for how to complete a timesheet, or how to make business-related travel plans. Simple guidance can be found in a checklist to help the worker remember the steps in the particular task. While you may not be able to write a procedure for everything, you can certainly improve on how clearly you have SET EXPECTATIONS.

WHY THIS BEHAVIOR OCCURRED—DIDN'T KNOW I SHOULD

If the Executives have not Set Expectations in a particular area, the employee may not know there is an expectation, rule, or policy in place and therefore may not know that they should do things a certain way. This may be a case where Vague Guidance has created confusion in the workforce and the employees simply don't know what they should be doing. If the employee didn't know they should do something, then you may have failed to clearly Set Expectations.

EXAMPLES OF PROACTIONS

CONDUCT paired observations with 10% of your leadership with a focus on their ability to communicate and reinforce safe work practices to their team.

AUDIT the documentation that guides how work is performed to ensure it is clear, easy to access, widely available, and free of conflicting guidance.

INTERVIEW a sample of employees (5%) to assess their understanding of the rules by asking them to explain the expectations for safe work; ensure what was said by leadership is what was heard by workers.

CONDUCT a series of *reverse briefings* where a junior member of the team leads the briefing and senior members critique the effectiveness of the plan. Use this interaction to assess if recent training of new hires aligns with the actual challenges of the work or if veteran members have drifted away from expected standards.

REVIEW the job-briefing form (or JSA, Job Safety Analysis) to ensure it isn't a check-the-box exercise and reinforces all safe work expectations.

HOW THE CULTURE SURVEY HELPS YOU MEASURE EFFECTIVENESS

A1a—Safety is the top priority at our company.

A1b—The company has established clear, written standards and expectations.

A1c—The company always looks for ways to improve how work is done.

A1d—The company's goals are routinely communicated to all employees.

If your employees would agree with these statements related to *Set Expectations,* you are on the right track.

SAFETY IS THE TOP PRIORITY AT OUR COMPANY (A1a)

Employees have a long memory and will discuss for years that one decision that placed production ahead of safety. Jimmy seemed to be treated differently a few days after he said the company was pushing too hard on the schedule, or Susan didn't get the promotion she was promised after she brought up a safety issue. It really doesn't matter whether these stories are accurate; at this point they've become part of the lore that is passed on to each new employee, and the story likely gets more egregious each time it is told. Even if you've made several good decisions that absolutely place safety as the top priority, they'll still be talking about that bad decision because they are not convinced (yet) that it won't happen again. If you don't have employee-led safety committees, you should do some benchmarking and put them in place. Consider open discussions, maybe on a weekly basis, with a cross-section of employees to hear what's on their minds and be sure to take good notes and follow up on the things you commit to do. Finally, take prompt action to address any decisions that appear to be putting safety behind anything else and give your employees some positive examples to share with the new hires.

THE COMPANY HAS ESTABLISHED CLEAR, WRITTEN STANDARDS AND EXPECTATIONS (A1b)

Many companies assume employees know what is expected, but never take the time to write it down to make sure that is the case. A plant manager recently said, "If you need a procedure to start up this plant then I don't want you working here." This is the wrong message. Procedures aren't there for you on your best day; they are there to help you on your worst. The problem is, you don't know whether today is going to be your best or your worst.

The underlying culprit when standards differ from crew to crew is that there are no written expectations in place. In this environment, everyone will do what they think is right, likely glad to be working at a place that lets them use their skills without the administrative burden of having to follow a procedure—until something goes wrong. When the weather is good, you have everything you need, and there is no pressure to get the job done quickly, most employees can complete any assigned task without incident. But what about when you are rushed to complete a task you haven't done in quite some time? That's where the value of written standards and expectations becomes most evident—because procedures are written to guide you through a task under the worst conditions—on your worst day.

If your company doesn't typically use procedures, consider taking a few of the most error-likely tasks that you do all the time and develop a checklist or basic procedure. If you see deviations in how the work is done across the organization, consider whether you've sufficiently communicated the standards to eliminate the variation. Write a policy statement that explains exactly what you want employees to do, or that clearly states your expectations. When employees have written guidance, they are more likely to meet your expectations because they know exactly what they are.

THE COMPANY ALWAYS LOOKS FOR WAYS TO IMPROVE HOW WORK IS DONE (A1c)

When things are going pretty well, it is easy to just keep doing things the way you are doing them. Why rock the boat? But companies with this mindset find themselves scrambling when the water gets a little rough. You should always be looking for ways to improve your efficiency and quality, and that means making minor changes when you see the need. If your night shift team is more efficient than your team on days, you should understand the difference and make necessary changes to improve performance. Maybe the results of your team at one site do not compare favorably with a team across town, or a facility in one state has solved an issue that has been a problem nationwide. These are occasions where you should take Warren Buffet's advice: "It is good to learn from your own mistakes, but it is better to learn from the mistakes of others."

If you don't have a process in place to capture lessons learned and good practices, you should develop one. The corrective actions taken to address a problem in one area should be shared broadly to minimize the risk of that event happening in another part of the company. Don't limit improvements to your inner circle—learn what other companies are doing to improve performance and take steps to consider similar actions in your company. Some highly resilient organizations (like nuclear plants and airlines) share lessons learned with competitors because they know one accident impacts the entire industry. Always look for best practices and share the lessons you've learned to prevent recurrence.

THE COMPANY'S GOALS ARE ROUTINELY COMMUNICATED TO ALL EMPLOYEES (A1d)

Years ago, company goals were posted on a bulletin board near the water cooler, and a surprising number of senior leaders think this technique still works. It clearly does not. If you don't believe this is true, just take a quick walk down the hall and see how many faded, outdated, and contradictory items are posted on your remaining bulletin boards. Communication of the company goals needs to be performed on a periodic basis using a variety of delivery methods to get the message out, including electronic media, video, and hardcopy handouts. The goals shouldn't be limited to a once-a-year presentation; they should be discussed throughout the year with updates on how the team is doing against the goals, with planned celebrations at key milestones. When performance is lagging, proactive steps should be taken to address the deviation with an action plan to get back on track. Progress and routine changes should be communicated to employees, and face-to-face sessions should be held occasionally with a sample of employees to hear directly from the workers.

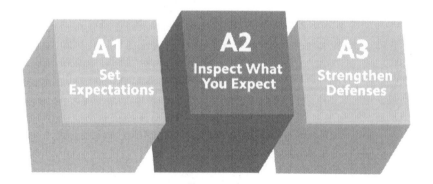

A2: INSPECT WHAT YOU EXPECT

FORMULA: Manage Change

MATRIX: Informed Executives

WHY THE BEHAVIOR OCCURRED: Not Important

Defining "Inspect What You Expect"

Executive engagement is critical to organizational success. Executives are responsible for the administration of Human Performance processes. Work activities are occasionally observed to ensure alignment with business strategies.

Why It's Important

Many people believe Human Performance is a priority only at the working level, where humans are performing tasks and sometimes making errors in the process. For the entire organization to be successful however, all employees—from the toolroom to the boardroom—must understand their role in organizational performance. Executive management sets the tone and direction for the organization so their role is critical to the success of any plan, including a company-wide approach to Human Performance. Their role in support of error-reduction initiatives is just as important as the role of those who are required to use these techniques in the field. "In fact, 70% of all strategic initiatives within an organization are doomed to fail because of misalignment amongst executives."[12] That means for every work week spent on organizational initiatives, 3.5 days are wasted."

This is a lesson we addressed in Part I. To be effective, Human Performance must be demonstrated and taught in the field—not just in the classroom. Another reason for in-field application is to combat how quickly you forget. Remember the Ebbinghaus Forgetting Curve from 1885, which shows a decline in knowledge retention of 67% within one day and 79% within three weeks after a one-time class? Probably not because...well, the Ebbinghaus Forgetting Curve. You must go in the field to see what is being remembered and applied.

How To Do It

Any initiative must begin by establishing a firm foundation for the change. The organization must determine why the change is necessary before developing a plan to implement the initiative. Communicating the details of the change is part of the information stage, where the new expectations are communicated to employees in a way that is easily understood. Application of the change requires a boots-on-the-ground approach involving in-field coaching and discussion. This leads to better retention of the information and greater productivity, as previously stated. When these steps are effectively applied, the organization will realize transformation as the change initiative becomes institutionalized in the culture.

Informed executives must make their own assessment of performance by personally observing work activities to ensure processes are being implemented as intended. Strategies for organizational performance improvement are designed and implemented, but without occasional monitoring and observation by executives these initiatives will become work as imagined misaligned with the strategy of the business where *work as imagined* is not consistent with *work as performed*. To supplement their personal observation, a system of performance indicators is used to monitor key aspects of business performance to allow proactive response.

While executives are responsible for setting the expectations, they also have the responsibility to make sure the expectations are understood and are being followed. Performance indicators, self-assessments and personal observation are used to ensure the expectations are being demonstrated throughout the organization and the intended organizational culture is healthy and vibrant.

Why The Behavior Occurred—Wasn't Important

You know there is a rule, but it seems optional since leadership doesn't follow it themselves, or never says anything about it when they see others not doing it.

Examples Of Proactions

IDENTIFY a recent change to how work should be performed (new JSA, introduction of HP, new tools or equipment, etc.) Observe five work activities that should adhere to this recent change to ensure the plan for work aligns with the performance of work.

REVIEW JSAs to determine if training for any recent changes to the work standards are being discussed in the field prior to work commencing.

ESTABLISH an observation process for your leadership to engage with workers in the field. Set clear expectations for the number and quality of observations to be performed each month.

CREATE a process for continuing training to prevent drift from expected standards. Determine how best to keep a constant trickle-flow of information that reinforces workplace standards and expectations.

ENSURE correct behaviors are being frequently and positively reinforced through incentive programs or public recognition.

How The Culture Survey Helps You Maintain Effectiveness

A2a—Activities are observed by someone in authority other than the direct supervisor.

A2b—Executives ensure company goals will be met by observing work activities.

A2c—The company is good at resolving problems.

A2d—Executives understand the challenges and concerns facing the workforce.

If your employees would agree with these statements related to *Inspect What You Expect,* you are on the right track:

ACTIVITIES ARE OBSERVED BY SOMEONE IN MANAGEMENT OTHER THAN THE DIRECT SUPERVISOR (A2a)

In many companies, a field visit from an Executive is like a drive-by shooting. They pass through the work area leaving a path of destruction in his or her wake, and everyone is glad when they are gone. The reason the field visit was such an event is because it is such a rare occurrence. Develop an internal observation plan that ensures leaders are out in the field on a recurring basis, so their presence does not become a spectacle. Workers should see the management team in their work area to, among other things, demonstrate their support of the Human Performance program.

EXECUTIVES ENSURE COMPANY GOALS WILL BE MET BY OBSERVING WORK ACTIVITIES (A2b)

This is the fundamental reason to inspect what you expect. The leadership team has set the goals for the company, but how can they know the activities in the field are aligned with the goals if they don't go see it for themselves? If the goals are to be met, reports from subordinates cannot be the only input that is received. There must be routine trips away from the corporate office and out into the spaces where the work is taking place. Remind yourself of the goals that have been set and --go to the field looking for evidence that the activities you observe are going to help the company be successful. Ask questions and get to know the workers, and make sure they know how their work is aligned with the goals.

The Company Is Good At Resolving Problems (A2c)

There are a multitude of problems at the working level--everything from paycheck issues, to parking, to availability of materials and vacant positions. It is unfortunate that most of these issues become part of the daily discussion because they never get fixed. Few issues rise to the level of resolution because they must go up the ladder for approval. Companies that have established a culture of fixing problems have several things in place:

- an effective reporting process,
- a method of prioritizing identified issues, and
- proportionate authority granted to resolve issues at the lowest level possible.

Clearly the big-ticket items need to be approved at higher levels, but in some companies the front-line leaders aren't entrusted with the authority to obtain basic supplies or solve routine issues until they get approval from their boss.

If you want your company to be efficient at resolving problems, consider whether you have any roadblocks in the way.

Executives Understand The Challenges And Concerns Facing The Workforce (A2d)

Many senior managers worked themselves up through the organization, some starting at the bottom. Others may have little experience in the technical aspects of the work but were selected for the position based on their leadership skills. Both cases present unique circumstances that may impact their ability to understand the daily challenges the workers face. If, for example, you've worked in the organization for a while, you'll likely remember your early days on the job. If that was 20 years ago, just think about how much has changed since then! The things that you complained about back then are a distant memory to today's workforce who must navigate electronic databases, passwords, and mobile apps just to get the basics done each day. If you think you know the challenges your workers are facing because you used to do the work yourself, consider whether the rapidly changing dynamics are impacting the credibility of your personal experience. Conversely, if you are the leader but haven't actually done the work, you may be getting your information on the concerns in the field from people who report to you. That's a good starting point, but they may have the same bias that we just illustrated. In either case, you'll never understand the challenges and concerns your workers are facing until you get to know them by talking to them and interacting with them in their work environment.

A3: STRENGTHEN DEFENSES

FORMULA: Error Defenses

MATRIX: Informed Executives

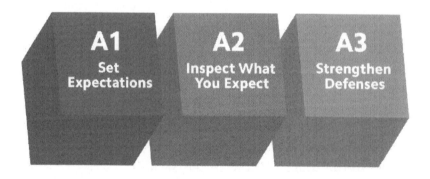

WHY THE BEHAVIOR OCCURRED: Didn't Know Why

Defining "Strengthen Defenses"

Executives use data to understand why gaps between standards and behaviors exist and take actions to mitigate risk. Design processes, procedures, and training to support error-free performance.

Why It's Important

Highly resilient organizations establish a culture of continuous improvement by maintaining a "preoccupation with failure."[13] This is particularly important in areas where operational errors can lead to consequential, if not devastating results, as in the airline industry, healthcare, or in nuclear facilities. In such environments where failure is not an option, the organization must demonstrate an unapologetically proactive bias toward action in the identification and resolution of Latent Organizational Weaknesses (LOWs). Executives who shun a continuous improvement approach as too robust or intended for only high-profile organizations do not understand the impact of establishing error defenses. Every organization should seek to continuously improve their performance through the reduction of errors, and this approach must be supported and communicated from the top levels of the company.

How To Do It

Many companies say employees are their most valuable asset, but few can back this statement up with their actions. A Gallup poll found that leaders in the top quartile engaged 77% of their employees on average, while leaders in the bottom quartile engaged only 1% of their employees.[14] Employee turnover remains high and employee errors persist, in part, due to insufficient training. While companies conduct periodic maintenance to ensure reliable and predictable equipment operation, employees rarely benefit from ongoing training programs to ensure their skill sets remain high. Employee development is often overlooked, leading to the promotion of employees to positions of leadership for which they have not been groomed, and their inevitable struggles in these positions. This is not the case in a learning organization where continuous improvement is embedded in the culture. The organizational churn, resulting from hiring new employees due to high turnover and replacement of leaders due to bad promotions, saps organizational momentum. A healthy, sustainable culture emerges when employee development and training become organizational priorities.

Potential risks are identified before they become self-revealing, allowing the organization to take proactive measures to deliver expected outcomes. Performance indicators are often used to provide an accurate, informed view of areas of focus. Astute executives will seek to understand the underlying trends in these indicators, asking targeted questions to ensure an aligned focus on agreed-upon corrective actions.

It's important to set priorities to ensure we are working on the most impactful areas for improvement, such as priority 1-3 or green, yellow and red categories. Performance indicators should monitor work as directed and not be based on STRETCH GOALS. A green indicator (indicating acceptable performance) should be determined based on obtainable goals that can be achieved by a highly performing team. In other words, green should not be unattainable, or require superhuman effort to achieve. Similarly, a yellow indicator (associated with off-track performance or an area for improvement) should be the subject of a corrective action plan to restore performance to the green band by a specific time, with an assigned owner and due date. A *red* indicator represents unacceptable performance and should be the subject of immediate actions and a formal plan to recover performance. In line with the mantra of "inspect what you expect," executives should pay particular attention to performance indicators as a primary method of assessing overall performance, informed by their personal observations of ongoing work in the field.

Why The Behavior Occurred—Didn't Know Why

Employees are often told WHAT to do, but rarely are they told WHY they are doing it. This leads to inconsistent performance because there is a lack of buy-in for the action and little commitment on the part of the employees.

Examples Of Proactions

SURVEY the workers to learn if the training program provides the knowledge and skills to meet the actual challenges of their work.

ESTABLISH organizational goals to encourage an increase in the reporting of near-misses and good catches. If no mechanism for reporting exists, or is not used, creating this process should be the priority.

SOLICIT employee feedback that is anonymous and focused on how to improve the performance of the organization. There are several online survey options available to help facilitate anonymous feedback or simply provide a paper form and drop box.

REVIEW any previous lessons learned and assess the effectiveness of the corrective actions taken. Communicate the response efforts so workers know that action is being taken and the organization is committed to improvement.

ASSESS the authority given to the first line supervisor to correct worksite related issues. Ensure they are appropriately enabled to quickly resolve worker concerns.

How The Culture Survey Helps You Measure Effectiveness

A3a—Executives anticipate problems and take actions to prevent them.

A3b—The company has a formal process in place to correct identified problems.

A3c—Employee development and training are important to the company.

A3d—Executives are always looking for ways to improve the company.

If your employees would agree with these statements related to *Strengthen Defenses*, you are on the right track.

EXECUTIVES ANTICIPATE PROBLEMS AND TAKE ACTION TO PREVENT THEM (A3a)

Senior leaders must look ahead to see what problems are on the horizon, taking proactive steps to minimize the impact on the company. Employees are focused on the short-term goals of meeting the daily schedule and satisfying customers, counting on the Executives to maintain a look-ahead view of company sustainability. When potential problems or disruptions become evident there needs to be a strong action plan in place to counter them. Performance indicators and other predictive tools can detect adverse trends to inform the development of corrective action plans. The expense of acting in a reactive manner, developing action plans after the problem is impacting the business, are always higher than the cost of taking proactive measures to minimize the impact.

THE COMPANY HAS A FORMAL PROCESS IN PLACE TO CORRECT IDENTIFIED PROBLEMS (A3b)

A formal process to document deficiencies is the only way to make sure they are prioritized, properly assigned, and tracked to closure. This also ensures the right emphasis is placed on the most important issues and allows the identification of trends before they become self-revealing. If you don't have a process in place to report deficiencies or latent organizational weaknesses, you are relying on good intentions and word-of-mouth to resolve these issues. Invariably, a handwritten note gets lost, or the issue is overcome by events and the deficiency lives on to impact your team on another day. Develop a simple database as a starting point to document, prioritize and assign identified problems.

EMPLOYEE DEVELOPMENT AND TRAINING ARE IMPORTANT TO THE COMPANY (A3c)

One of the most frequent complaints of workers is that they don't get enough training. This is often quite a surprise to Executives who look at the number of hours of training they've provided and can't reconcile the issue they are hearing with what they've approved. The issue isn't that they haven't had numerous hours of training; it is that the training they had isn't what they needed to be better on the job. Many of the approved hours for annual training are taken up by required safety classes and various administrative topics. Few hours are focused on the technical skills the workers need to do their job, and that is the training they want to get that leads to the complaints. Similarly, top performers are given little time to prepare before they are expected to step into the new role. Like training, employee development should be a management priority. Ideally workers would be groomed for intended promotions and given an opportunity to work in the shadow of experienced leaders who can show them the ropes. In fact, Millennials (45%) are far more likely than Gen-Xers (31%) or baby boomers (18%) to say that a job that accelerates their professional or career development is "very important" to them.[15] As people move up within the organization, they will need to expand their people-skills, and this should be taken into consideration when promotions are considered. Just because an employee is the best performer at a technical task doesn't mean they are the best choice to lead a team of people that perform that task.

EXECUTIVES ARE ALWAYS LOOKING FOR WAYS TO IMPROVE THE COMPANY (A3d)

When it comes to making organizational improvements, everyone has a part to play. As presented in the REMEDY Matrix, employees should communicate their concerns, leaders should listen and correct the identified issues, and executives should develop a culture of continuous improvement which allows these interactions to occur as a normal part of doing business. Establishing a culture of trust where information passes through all levels of the organization is not easy to do because trust is fragile and one bad decision will set you back. It takes time, but it is a critically important part of your role. Consider an executive (who has not built a culture of trust) who comes up with an idea that will improve the company. Employees may be skeptical, thinking the improvement will simply serve to pad his annual bonus at their expense. The same idea, presented to an organization that believes in the management of the company and trusts their intentions, will be received much differently. Always look for ways to improve the work conditions, the delivery of training, the processes, and the facilities. When possible, get the employees involved at the front end and listen to their ideas to strengthen the level of trust.

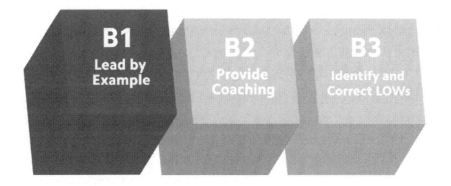

SECTION II

EMPOWERED LEADERS

B1: LEAD BY EXAMPLE

FORMULA: Reduce Error

MATRIX: Empowered Leaders

WHY THE BEHAVIOR OCCURRED: Wasn't Accountable

Defining "Lead By Example"

Leaders communicate their expectations for the team to minimize risk. Leaders understand and demonstrate the appropriate use of error reduction techniques.

Why It's Important

Most change initiatives rise and fall at the frontline leadership level. Their commitment and buy-in is critical to the success of Human Performance within your organization. Think about how much influence leaders have in an organization's culture. While the executives may decide that Human Performance is going to be part of the organization's culture, the leaders are the ones who can see, every day, if this is actually happening. Your workers are also taking their cues from their field leadership. Workers are already skeptical about anything new and are judging how seriously they need to take any directives from on high. If their leadership is not leading by example then the workers are led to believe that it must not be important, so why bother?

Think about the worker who is *all in* on Human Performance but has a first-line supervisor *who is not* leading by example. The worker certainly isn't in the position to coach or challenge their supervisor. They are simply watching and assessing how serious they are about change. If the leader is apathetic towards Human Performance, you can almost guarantee that the employees will not be engaged. Even if the Executive level is championing Human Performance, a leader who is not setting a good example will provide cover for the people working under them to also not participate.

The first-line leadership will either lead the change, or inadvertently lead the resistance through inaction.

126

How To Do It

Whether good or bad, the actions of leaders are contagious. The leader has a complex role in ensuring company success, walking a fine line between work production and profit, and generating a positive culture that values employee engagement. Leaders that are overly focused on production will eventually be surrounded by team members who share the same values, likely suppressing the views of employees who would like to speak up but may feel it is not wise to do so. The company values should describe desired workplace behaviors such as valuing employee feedback, acting with integrity, placing a priority on safety, and working productively.

Leaders should demonstrate all these values all the time, and through their example should encourage employees to act in accordance with the company values as well. This, of course, is easier said than done. "Over 1000 leaders participated in an assessment in 2022 and only 27.4% of them said "leading by example" was their greatest leadership strength."[16]

When leaders *lead by example* in a positive way, they are strengthening an organizational culture that effectively balances concern for the bottom line with concern for the employees; both are important in the reduction of errors.

Why The Behavior Occurred—Wasn't Accountable

You know there is a rule, but it seems optional since leadership doesn't follow it themselves, or never says anything about it when they see others not doing it.

EXAMPLES OF PROACTIONS

OBSERVE employees performing assigned tasks and assess whether they have the necessary guidance documents to do the work safely and efficiently.

PERFORM paired observations with jobsite supervision to assess the leader's ability to model the expected behaviors to give their team a clear vision of what good looks like.

SURVEY frontline supervisors to identify the conditions that make performing work as prescribed in job planning difficult to execute in the field. Center the discussion around specific rules that trending has identified as disconnected from worker behaviors.

PROVIDE on-the-job, in the field, or jobsite training (versus classroom or online) for skills that have been identified as not conforming to organizational expectations. This will create a clearer vision for the worker to apply the correct behaviors to their specific job.

ASK the workers and frontline supervisors to develop a new employee training plan. This should reveal their prioritization of current workplace standards and allow for either a resetting of their understanding or a shift in training emphasis.

HOW THE CULTURE SURVEY HELPS YOU MEASURE EFFECTIVENESS

B1a—Leaders never encourage anyone to bypass the rules.

B1b—Leaders model the right behaviors and lead by example.

B1c—Leaders act in a way that reflects the company's values.

B1d—Leaders clearly communicate their expectations.

If your employees would agree with these statements related to *Lead by Example,* you are on the right track:

LEADERS NEVER ENCOURAGE ANYONE TO BYPASS THE RULES (B1a)

Often it is the new employee who brings up a procedure or policy reference because they have recently read about something as part of their orientation. The way you respond has long-lasting implications for that employee and for those who are watching from a distance. Let's say you are sending the teams out to do the scheduled work and a new employee notes that you didn't do the required checklists to make sure the material and equipment is ready. You say it is OK because the teams will complete their checks once they get to the job location. He shows you the procedure that says the checklist is to be completed before departing. Your employees are waiting for your response. Will you belittle the employee for bringing this up, or will you recognize him for holding a high standard for procedural adherence? This is a simple example, but it may point to a pervasive mindset of *get the job done* rather than one that questions, "What does the procedure say?"

If the rules and procedures aren't right, then take the time to correct them—don't work around them.

LEADERS MODEL THE RIGHT BEHAVIORS AND LEAD BY EXAMPLE (B1b)

Maybe it is just human nature, but most of the workers who report to you will determine their level of professionalism based on the example you have set. If you have high standards then they are likely to rise to your standard, but conversely, if you have a bad attitude or routinely cut corners, your team will follow suit. Either way, you are leading by example. How can you expect your employees to be on time for meetings if you are routinely late yourself? What if you roll through stop signs, don't wear a seat belt, and text while you are driving? Your credibility takes a hit when you talk to your employees about safe driving. As a leader, you should demonstrate the behaviors you expect of your team.

LEADERS ACT IN A WAY THAT REFLECTS THE COMPANY'S VALUES (B1c)

Company values often include character, trust, dependability, and integrity. Some include curiosity, fun and flexibility. When you accepted the promotion to become a leader, you become even more accountable to upholding the company values and demonstrating them in your actions. Do you know what your company values are? If not, how can you know you are acting in a way that reflects them? Take the time to review the company values and commit yourself to living in accordance with them.

LEADERS CLEARLY COMMUNICATE THEIR EXPECTATIONS (B1d)

Many times, when employees are interviewed after an incident, it becomes obvious that they didn't know what to do because the expectations were not clear. A policy conflicts with a procedure that differs from the direction the employee got at turnover. Something as simple as using PPE can be confusing if not clearly communicated. What is my required PPE, where can I get it, when is it necessary, and how do I properly use it? Any amount of confusion can lead to employee disengagement, increasing error rates, and a decline in productivity, and many of the employees not knowing what is expected of them. Maybe the leader doesn't know the expectations and is just doing the best they can each day. This is a fundamental premise of Reducing Errors within the REMEDY Matrix: Executives set the expectations, Leaders demonstrate them, and Employees follow them. You should be keenly aware of any *gray area* in your expectations because you want everyone to know *what good looks like.* It is the job of a leader to clearly communicate what is expected, so there is no confusion.

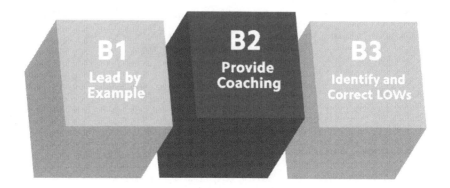

B2: PROVIDE COACHING

FORMULA: Manage Change

MATRIX: Empowered Leaders

WHY THE BEHAVIOR OCCURRED: Didn't Know How

DEFINING "PROVIDE COACHING"

Coaching is provided to help employees align with and contribute to the overall values of the company. Positive reinforcement is used to encourage a culture of trust.

WHY IT'S IMPORTANT

Some leaders feel they don't have time to coach employees as they are busy with meetings and other activities and just can't find the time to get involved. A Personnel Management Association internal report[17] showed that when training is combined with coaching, employees increased their productivity by an average of 86% compared to 22% with training alone. Either due to conflicting priorities or lack of communication, many leaders may have a narrow view of their role in achieving the goals of the organization. In fact, leaders who are aligned with the goals of the company and feel empowered to meet them view employee coaching as a *must do* instead of a *nice to do.*

For example:

Employee coaching is an important tool in developing talent in organizations where competition for good workers is a daily struggle. Replacing workers, either due to poor hiring practices or lack of development, is a costly endeavor for the company.

Coaching allows the leader to get a first-hand view of the work conditions so prompt changes can be implemented to make processes more efficient. This has a direct impact on the bottom line and generates a culture of continuous improvement.

Leaders building relationships with employees is good business, and effective coaching provides a vehicle for this interaction. Research shows that 75% of workers considered their direct boss to be "the worst part of their job" and 65% would rather have a new boss than a pay raise.[18] Coaching interactions allow leaders to build relationships with their team and strengthen morale.

Leaders who spend time with their employees will have a better understanding of developing misalignments between the company goals and employee understanding of them. Proactive steps can be taken to address these developing gaps before they become a problem. Periodic coaching and employee interaction allows the conversations that reveal these gaps to take place.

When employees receive encouraging words from their leaders, they feel valued and appreciated and are more likely to stay. Most people leave the company due to bad management, often demonstrated through a lack of interaction. A recent survey found that 65% of workers received no recognition of any kind in the last year.[19] Coaching provides an avenue for recognition and allows a recurring opportunity to provide positive feedback and build a culture of trust within the organization.

132

How To Do It

True leadership is an elusive goal that many will never realize. It is a level of recognition that is more than a title, as many have a title but are woeful leaders. It's kind of like the saying, *just because you are standing in the garage, that doesn't make you a car.* The same is true of leadership, regardless of your title. A first-line supervisor, recently promoted, may be reading articles on whether leaders are born that way, or if they can learn how to lead. This is a good approach, and one of the most frequently asked of professional management coaches. The truth is the organization should have been developing the potential supervisor long before their promotion. An assessment of an employee's skills and vulnerabilities would inform the development plan so they could step right into the new role with confidence instead of being overwhelmed by it. This begs the question, "are leaders born that way or can they be taught how to lead?"

If you think about a bell curve, you realize there are 15% or so of people who are born with the natural talent to step right into roles of leadership. They have the necessary vision and the right amount of charisma to lead. Primarily, they are self-aware, know their strengths and weaknesses, and are willing to receive feedback that is used to close existing gaps in their performance. At the other end of the curve are those who are not born to lead, and don't want to. They are comfortable in the role of *doer* and may be exceptionally good at it. In fact, many organizations complain about the loss of good workers but often the damage is self-imposed as super doers are promoted to supervisor. This often leads to failure because the skill set of a good worker is vastly different from the skill set of a supervisor, and if you don't prepare them for the promotion you are asking for trouble. That leaves the broad range of employees residing under the steepest part of the bell curve— those who can be trained to be leaders. You need to assess their capabilities, develop a training plan that addresses their vulnerabilities, and provide opportunities for them to gradually step into leadership roles so they can prove themselves and gain confidence. Employees in this category might not demonstrate the attributes of a good leader, and that's OK. At least you know you have a good *doer* on your hands rather than promoting them and watching them fail.

It is surprising how many supervisors have had no formal training in leadership. There is no assessment, no development plan, and no opportunities to shadow another leader. Is it any wonder that a recent survey by the Corporate Executive Board found that 60% of new managers will fail in the first 24 months? [20] A popular book on this subject is *The Leadership Pipeline,*[21] which describes the different leadership transitions from an individual contributor being promoted for the first time, to the transitions that occur as leaders are promoted to the senior levels of the organization. Of course, the transition into the first level of leadership involves a change in mindset from doing the job to leading those who do it. This seems like an easy transition to make (especially if you are in the 15% that are seemingly born to lead) but it is of fundamental importance because a failure to make this necessary transition will impact every transition that follows. In fact, it may be a hurdle to any further advancement and may ultimately be a new leader's undoing.

As a leader ascends through the organization their people-skills must improve along the way, because the farther removed you are from the individual contributor role, the less important your technical skills become. Accordingly, the importance of development training for new leaders cannot be understated. They don't need a philosophical or academic approach to this training—they just need to know what to expect, and how to think like a leader instead of a worker.

Coaching is such an important part of any change initiative. Learning how to be an effective coach not only benefits a Human Performance change initiative but will help leaders in all aspects of their job. The COACH acronym is a good place to start:

COMMUNICATE YOUR EXPECTATIONS

A recent survey found that 69% of managers are uncomfortable communicating with their employees.[22] Considering that communication is one of the most important attributes of a leader, this number is particularly troublesome. There are several reasons why your communications often fail. One reason is that you make a vague declaration, but there is no call to action—you assume compliance without asking for agreement.[23] It's like the weather report you see on the news on Sunday night. You know that there is a strong possibility that what the weatherman says about Friday's weather is probably not going to be perfectly accurate. You listen, but don't take the information very seriously. Similarly, when you state an expectation early in the week, be sure your team understands that you are making an assignment, not a casual delegation. Otherwise, when the team doesn't meet your expectation, a team member will likely say, "I didn't realize your statement was a request. I thought you were just talking."

Another reason communications fail is because the leader fears saying the wrong thing or saying it the wrong way. This often leads to complex communication protocols that attempt to cover every possible angle while leaving the real message buried under long-winded attempts to make the message clear. Don't assume you have to talk down to your employees or coworkers to get your message across, or that you have to go overboard with elaborate explanations of what you want. Just explain it plainly and then listen to their response for additional clarification that may be required.

OBSERVE BEHAVIORS

Most observations are focused on counting occasions of noncompliance. That guy isn't wearing gloves, that lady over there is using the wrong procedure, and the new employee isn't wearing a seatbelt. By the end of the week, you have four employees who were observed not wearing gloves, and now you have your theme for the next work week—people aren't wearing gloves, so that becomes the focus. OK, you've identified several cases of noncompliance, and of course you want to have fewer observations like these, but WHY aren't they wearing gloves, or for that matter, WHY aren't employees wearing seatbelts? When you ask deeper questions, you are getting to the behavior that leads to noncompliance and that puts you in good shape to really fix the issue.

Let's say you have a roach problem in your kitchen and your spouse calls for your assistance. You get rid of the roach, but you should know the problem is potentially much bigger because if you see one roach out in the open, there are probably dozens more in the dark, out-of-the-way spaces. Compliance-based observations are like killing one roach at a time; your effort is effective on a limited basis and in the short term. That's why you need to base your observations on behaviors, not compliance. If you see a worker without gloves, interact with that person and inquire why they are not wearing the gloves that are required. Listen carefully to the answer and start to think about the behavior that contributes to the noncompliance. Maybe the policy is vague, and the employee doesn't know whether or not gloves are required. Maybe the correct gloves (either size or design) are not available so the staff member has to decide whether to proceed as best they can, or whether it would be best to stop and get the right PPE. Maybe the worker's gloves are in their locker but felt like there was not enough time to go all the way back to get them.

All of these questions are getting to the behavior, and the mindset, which lead to the observed noncompliance. Is Time Pressure a contributor? Is the expectation unclear, allowing wide variation in what people actually do? If you determine the behaviors are primarily due to Time Pressure, then by focusing on this distraction (rather than the number of times you were noncompliant related to glove use) you are solving problems you didn't even know you had. Consider the new employee who may not be wearing his seatbelt due to Time Pressure—he was just in a hurry and forgot about it. When you have a compliance-based observation program it is easy to meet the weekly quota because non-compliance issues are easy to see (like the roach in the kitchen). It is more difficult to see behaviors because you won't see them unless you are looking for them.

Acknowledge Positive Behavior

Managers often don't like giving constructive feedback, and multiple surveys consistently show the following reasons: 1) They lack confidence. 2) They don't like confrontation. But what about positive feedback? A lack of confidence is a hurdle regardless of the type of feedback, and in the case of giving positive feedback, many leaders don't recognize the powerful impact of recognizing performance and motivating employees to meet expectations. Often trapped by past experiences, they somehow view the delivery of positive feedback as something that makes them look weak, and this is very unfortunate. Positive feedback is critically important, especially in the early stages of learning.

In development of a research paper in 2012, a survey was conducted of students in introductory French classes, and of those in advanced courses in French literature.[24] The students were asked which type of instructor they preferred—one who emphasized what students were doing well in the class and discussed their strengths, or an instructor who focused mostly on what mistakes they made and how to fix them. The students who were new to French overwhelmingly wanted the instructor who gave positive feedback, and those with more experience wanted an instructor who would correct the mistakes they made. This experiment shows that as people gain experience in a subject, the role of feedback serves a different purpose.

Many employees and leaders are novices in Human Performance, still learning the terms and techniques to reduce errors and injuries on the job. Because they lack a depth of experience, they need to hear encouraging words about what they are doing right, so they will keep doing it. When you observe someone performing in accordance with your expectations, you should take the time to acknowledge this positive behavior in a credible and sincere way. A good rule of thumb is to give positive feedback four times more than constructive, corrective feedback.

CHANGE MANAGEMENT

When it comes right down to it, you are a creature of habit.

Even with some evidence that a change will make things work better, you often resist that change because you would rather keep the current system or process (remember the Culture Cycle) than to go through the hassle of transitioning to something new. You've figured out how to work within the current system, so you'd rather just keep it the way it is. How many have declined a software update because they were wary of the uncertainties the update would bring? This behavior is all too common, and there are reasons for it. First, you sense a loss of control. People generally don't like to support changes they didn't have any voice in creating. A wise manager will invite others into the planning process, giving them a sense of ownership of the change. Another reason people resist change is because they think the change will create more work for them, and they are often right. That's why it's important to get a good start on any organizational change, with alignment and understanding of the reason for the change. After the attention placed on the new project starts to fade, some will start looking for a new shiny object upon which to dedicate their time and energy. This is referred to as "Kanter's Law," [25] which states that everything looks like failure in the middle, but that is where the hard work takes place!

An effective leader will understand the need for the change, expecting some level of resistance from subordinates, but be able to speak directly to their concerns. First-line supervisors are especially important in managing change and should be involved in preplanning activities before a change initiative is launched. They not only need to know what the change is and why it is being implemented, but they must also ensure their employees understand the plan and support the change.

Help Workers Succeed

While leaders may understand the value of their presence in the field with their workers, they rarely make the time to spend with them. The most frequently heard excuse is, "I have too many meetings." Some organizations have tried to correct this problem by scheduling management observations in the field or establishing a quota of so many field visits that must be accomplished each month. Such efforts, although well-intentioned, often do not result in effective, beneficial interactions with employees. Employees see the boss coming from a mile away and often take an extended break until the periodically required *time in the field* has passed. The workers are glad to see him leave and know they won't see him again until this time next month. But what if you could change the interaction management has with the workers into something they look forward to? Instead of being glad the leader is leaving, what if the employees appreciated the visit so much, they encouraged the boss to come back again soon? The only way to make this transition is for the leader to listen to the employees and act on their concerns. A periodic visit to meet a quota and check off a box is not going to do it.

The actions under the COACH acronym are meant to strengthen the effectiveness of management observations and to improve relationships, and that is why the "H" in COACH is so important. When a leader helps the workers by understanding the concerns they face each day and removing roadblocks that are preventing the efficient conduct of their duties, that leader is strengthening organizational performance. Consider asking your employees to tell you one thing that you can do to make them safer and more effective on the job, then just listen. Don't overcommit by promising things you can't deliver but pick one thing that is within your power to accomplish and focus on that item. Take the necessary actions to eliminate the problem, and then be sure to give the employees feedback on what has been done. Small wins such as these will increase trust, improve morale, and provide opportunities for additional conversations and more open dialogue. *Check the box* management observations often do more harm than good.

WHY THE BEHAVIOR OCCURRED—DIDN'T KNOW HOW

Employees may be aware of the general rule, but they haven't been given any coaching or training to understand the specific technical actions they should be taking.

EXAMPLES OF PROACTIONS

PERFORM paired observations with an emphasis on assessing the leader's ability to maintain their oversight role and not become distracted by engaging in the performance of the work.

UTILIZE any incentive programs to provide positive reinforcement for behaviors that meet or exceed workplace standards. Set specific goals for your leaders to utilize the incentive processes provided.

COMMUNICATE with your team three to five examples of when the correct behaviors, aligned with organizational standards, prevented or reduced the severity of an accident or error.

CONDUCT a 180-degree assessment of your leaders (this is when the leader submits their own assessment of their job performance) specifically targeted at their ability to coach their workers. This should reveal areas where your leaders may need further training.

REVIEW the training process for your new leaders to assess if they are given guidance to help them with the skill of coaching.

This is an opportunity to determine if leaders are being asked to coach without being given training or mentoring in this new skill.

HOW THE CULTURE SURVEY HELPS YOU TO MEASURE EFFECTIVENESS

B2a—Leaders seek to understand the employee's point of view.

B2b—Leaders hold employees accountable to standards and expectations.

B2c—Leaders actively develop employees by providing specific, constructive feedback.

B2d—Leaders provide positive reinforcement of proper behaviors.

If your employees would agree with these statements related to *Provide Coaching,* you are on the right track:

LEADERS SEEK TO UNDERSTAND THE EMPLOYEE'S POINT OF VIEW (B2a)

As a leader you have a better overall view of performance and can make more informed decisions about what needs to be done, but you shouldn't do it alone. Make sure you are having routine meetings with a sample of your employees to get their perspective and hear their concerns. On these occasions you should share with them a few of the ideas you have in mind and get their thoughts on them. Consider various means of soliciting employee feedback, either from occasional meetings as discussed, a suggestion drop box, or a group chat format where employees can voice their concerns or ideas. Listen with an open mind and make changes according to the feedback you get, especially when you hear it from several people. Value employee input and consider their point of view when making decisions that directly impact them.

LEADERS HOLD EMPLOYEES ACCOUNTABLE TO STANDARDS AND EXPECTATIONS (B2b)

One of the biggest complaints from employees is that they are having to do more than their share of the work because management won't hold the other workers accountable to do their part. At least that's the way they explain it. This makes for a disgruntled workforce—one which good employees will eventually leave. The first step to take is to make sure the expectations are clear because if everyone is held to the same standard, then the outliers become more evident. One mistake that leaders often make is to *paint everyone with the same brush*—meaning they don't have the courage to confront a worker who is not meeting the standard, so they resort to the comfort of a group meeting to provide the necessary feedback when there is only one person who needs to hear it. And everyone in the room knows who that person is, and now they know that you have taken the easy route instead of having the one-on-one discussion that is necessary. Don't equate accountability with punishment, because the two are quite different. When an employee is not meeting a clearly communicated standard, they need to be *coached* back to compliance. They should *expect to be held accountable* for their performance when it deviates from the standard. When an employee is repeatedly out of compliance with a standard, and discussions and coaching are not having a positive impact on their behavior, discipline is warranted. This result differs from accountability.

LEADERS ACTIVELY DEVELOP EMPLOYEES BY PROVIDING SPECIFIC, CONSTRUCTIVE FEEDBACK (B2c)

When not delivered properly, constructive feedback is just criticism if it isn't focused on behavior. Telling an employee they are irresponsible will not help them improve because you haven't presented a behavior that needs to be addressed. Your comment is neither specific, nor constructive. However, if you tell them the days they came in late in the last week, then they have something on which they can focus. Be sure you aren't using your words to tear someone down as if you are burning a bridge instead of building one. Look for opportunities to develop your employees by discussing their opportunities for growth rather than a list of their failures.

If you consider every interaction with your employees as a way to actively improve their performance, your feedback will become more constructive because they will receive it as part of their development and not as emotional criticism.

LEADERS PROVIDE POSITIVE REINFORCEMENT OF PROPER BEHAVIORS (B2d)

Many leaders find difficulty in providing positive feedback because they grew up in an environment where it was rare. They tend to think that *no news is good news* as their experience has been that feedback is always focused on criticisms. They have a push mentality, defined by setting deadlines and driving others to accomplish the company goals. Consider the converse, where a leader gets employees excited about a goal and inspires them to meet it. They recognize the team, rewarding high performance and are generous with their praise. They are out in front pulling the team to victory. To be honest, there must be a balance of push and pull in any organization, but the value of positive feedback is often unrecognized. If you find yourself in a group of leaders who are not exceptionally good at giving positive feedback, don't let that discourage you. Show your support for this guidance by committing to giving two positive comments per day. After a week or so raise the number to three and so on. Be honest with your employees that you want to change in this area and look for opportunities to encourage workers by recognizing their good efforts, no matter how small. Be sincere and timely in your delivery of positive feedback and you will raise the level of trust within the organization.

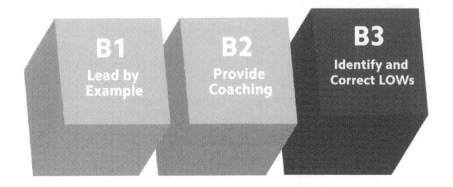

B3: Identify and Correct LOWs

Formula: Error Defenses

Matrix: Empowered Leaders

Why the behavior occurred: Can't

Defining "Identify And Correct Latent Organizational Weaknesses"

Latent Organizational Weaknesses (LOWs) are identified, prioritized, and eliminated. Employees are encouraged to identify LOWs and leadership communicates resolutions.

Why It's Important

Latent Organizational Weaknesses (LOWs) are undetected deficiencies in processes, equipment or values that create job-site conditions that either provoke error or degrade the integrity of controls. It is simpler to describe LOWs as snakes in the grass that are lying in wait for an unsuspecting passer-by.

Consider the board game Jenga. As pieces are removed from the tower of blocks it becomes more and more unstable and that instability can easily be seen by the players. But what about the view from above? The view from the top looks solid, sturdy, and complete. If you only look at the Jenga tower from a top-down view, it never changes from the moment the tower is built to the moment before it collapses. You can easily be lulled into a position of complacency because from your point of view everything is fine, even if there are growing weaknesses in the structure that are outside of your view.

This is the impact LOWs have on organizational performance, but unlike Jenga where everyone is in competition with one another, you are all in this together. You all should identify organizational weaknesses and feel responsible when latent issues are identified and left uncorrected. What do you do when you identify inaccurate training materials? What about a broken tool that is returned to the toolbox? What action do you take when a print or procedure contains an error? Each of these scenarios represents latent organizational weaknesses. Empowered leaders are trained to identify such issues and place the right priority on their resolution.

Nearly 12% of all hospital patients in a recent British study experienced an adverse event during their stay, with one-third of these events leading to disability ranging from moderate to severe, including death. Researchers determined half of these events could have been prevented with ordinary standards of care, and organizational weaknesses were found to be at the root of each problem. Consider: In a review of 6770 infusion / transfusion related accidents and injuries, over a ten-year period, the Medicines and Healthcare Products Regulatory Agency found that 54% of the cases were related to user error; the equipment was found to be in good condition, but the staff didn't know how to use the device. Supporting this statistic, the FDA found that 27% of medical devices are designed without adequate consideration of the end user and human factor issues.[26] When one person doesn't understand how to use equipment, it might be due to missed training or an individual's lack of competence. When 54% of the users are having trouble using the equipment, it might be a latent organizational weakness in the design of the equipment, or the training provided.

Workers are pretty adept at working around latent organizational weaknesses. This is what keeps these problems flying under the radar. Workers either never notice the problem or they figure out how to deal with them and just move one. Either way, the issue is never reported and corrected. When a worker does take the time and effort to point out an organizational weakness, leaders must take action to not only correct the problem, but to encourage more people to speak up.

How To Do It

Employees are often the ones having to deal with LOWs daily, therefore they should be trained to recognize LOWs so they can be corrected rather than passed on to the next unsuspecting coworker. As a learning organization, the resolution of LOWs should be communicated so others will be aware of the issue, know how it was corrected, and be encouraged to adopt a similar focus on identification and resolution of LOWs.

The concept of *employee silence* was introduced in 1974, addressing the reasons employees don't speak up when they are aware of organizational problems (Including fear of isolation, embarrassment, reluctance to implicate coworkers, and the feeling that they don't have an avenue to voice their opinion.). As J. Aylsworth explains in a 2008 article for www.examiner.com, a *silent employee* will often concede and thereby normalize an unwanted organizational condition. Therefore, it is important for the empowered leader to understand the nature of latent organizational weaknesses sufficiently to teach others. Part of this instruction must include a discussion on why it's important to identify and report such issues, and how to do so.

Why The Behavior Occurred—Can't

Employees cannot follow the rule due to physical constraints, a lack of equipment, materials, resources, procedures, or other guidance.

Examples Of Proactions

CONDUCT field observations to determine if workers are actively utilizing a Questioning Attitude to assess emergent issues and the need to stop and regroup.

DEVELOP communication to the employees to reinforce the expectation that productivity is good—it keeps you employed— but that safety is paramount and productivity pressure will not be tolerated. Don't rush to get the job done despite safety.

ASSESS the current Stop Work policy to determine if it is effective. Report on the frequency that workers utilize Stop Work authority. Most companies have a policy that is seldom used; determine if your organization has room for improvement in this area.

ASSIGN one member of each crew or work team to be the "devil's advocate." This person should productively question elements of the work plan as the rest of the team defends the completeness of their plan. Document any issues that could not be definitively confirmed.

VALIDATE the JSA process by having 3-5 JSAs completed and briefed by upper management. This should give the executive level good insight into the challenges of the current system utilized by their workers.

How The Culture Survey Helps You Measure Effectiveness

B3a—Leaders quickly resolve issues.

B3b—Leaders have the authority to correct issues that impact job performance.

B3c—Leaders encourage employees to identify and report work-related issues.

B3d—When an event occurs, we take the right actions to make sure it doesn't happen again.

If your employees would agree with these statements related to *Identify and Correct LOWs*, you are on the right track.

LEADERS QUICKLY RESOLVE ISSUES (B3a)

It has been said that all of life is problem solving, and that's what leaders inherently do. Recognizing the potential for problems and then attacking them before they become consequential sustains momentum in the organization by preventing setbacks resulting from a reactive response. But you have many distractions that prevent you from taking proactive steps to minimize problems and that is where good leaders separate themselves from the pack. Problem solving must be maintained as a priority, even when employee issues are demanding your time, or administrative burdens seem too great. Despite these distractions, your team is still dealing with the problem and that is impacting their effectiveness, and eventually their morale. They are looking to the leader to resolve the issues they've identified. Of course, there must be some prioritization so you spend your time on the most impactful problems, and the bigger issues could take more time to resolve as you may have to work with others to find a solution. The key is to address the issues in a timely manner, communicate your plans, and not get distracted, allowing problems to linger. Your team is counting on you to resolve these issues.

LEADERS HAVE THE AUTHORITY TO CORRECT ISSUES THAT IMPACT JOB PERFORMANCE (B3b)

Many leaders find themselves in a difficult position because they encourage workers to identify problems, but then the leader must get permission from his or her supervisor before any actions are taken. This causes unnecessary delays in resolving problems and creates frustration at the working level as things get lost in the *black hole* as it is passed up the ladder. Leaders should be granted the authority to address issues that are impacting performance without having to ask for permission every time. There are clearly monetary limits that may need to be established, or occasions where a policy change will need upper management engagement, but in most cases the closest leader to the work should be able to make the necessary decisions. As described in the Matrix, Empowered Leaders *are entrusted with the authority* to act on worker feedback.

LEADERS ENCOURAGE EMPLOYEES TO IDENTIFY AND REPORT WORK-RELATED ISSUES (B3c)

The workers know what the problems are that are impacting their performance. They see the time that is wasted driving across town to get a work order, filling out forms that add no value, or reordering materials that they know are not the best choice. You need to encourage workers to speak up when they see areas for improvement rather than going through the motions. But how do you do that? Many of you have workers who would be glad to waste two hours driving around town or ordering substandard materials because they are just doing what you told them to do. This represents malicious compliance where the workers follow your strict orders, but know it is not the right action for the company. In other words, you need to get them engaged in what you are trying to do, so you gain the benefit of their thoughts and ideas and not just the physical work they can do. If you can get your employees to understand the big-picture goals of the company, and report issues that are adversely impacting these goals, you will be on the right track to improving performance across the board. Leaders should be receptive to employee feedback because negative reactions will have a long-lasting impact. If a worker reports a cut on his finger, you should take the necessary immediate actions but should view this as an opportunity to prevent a much worse accident down the road. The same approach is warranted when employees identify procedural inaccuracies, incorrect postings, or policy inconsistencies.

WHEN AN EVENT OCCURS, WE TAKE THE RIGHT ACTIONS TO MAKE SURE IT DOESN'T HAPPEN AGAIN (B3d)

Too often your focus is on what it is going to take to address an unfortunate issue so you can get back to work. Predictable corrective actions from leaders with this mindset are 1) talk to the employees in a morning meeting or stand down, and 2) add the topic to the agenda in your next training session. Aside from dishing out some level of discipline as deemed necessary, that's about it—problem solved. A few months later the same event happens again, and the leader thinks about how to make the morning meeting more effective this time around. But the morning meeting is not the problem—the approach is the problem. If you clearly understand the event, you can develop much more effective corrective actions—or as Charles Kettering, the famed inventor, and head of research for GM once said, "a problem well-stated is half-solved." When developing a corrective action plan, think about actions that are necessary to solve the immediate issue but consider actions that will prevent recurrence as well. For example, let's say an employee was injured after a fall in the parking lot. The easy action to take would be to tell everyone to be more careful. But were there contributors to the accident, like inadequate lighting, or no designated walkways? If your investigation determines lighting was a direct contributor, the first action should be to install a light to eliminate this concern. But to determine the extent of the condition, you should look at the other parking lots and walkways to see if there are other dimly lit areas where a similar accident could occur. What about your other locations, across town or far away? You should share the event and your corrective action plan with them to make sure they aren't vulnerable to a similar accident at their site.

ENGAGED EMPLOYEES

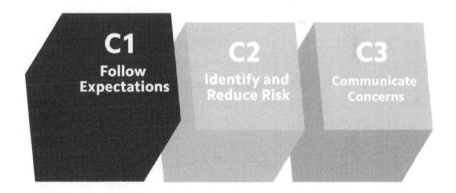

C1: FOLLOW EXPECTATIONS

FORMULA: Reduce Errors

MATRIX: Engaged Employees

WHY THE BEHAVIOR OCCURRED: Forgot

DEFINING "FOLLOW EXPECTATIONS"

All tasks are performed in accordance with policies, procedures, and expectations. Decisions are made considering unwanted consequences and how to control and mitigate risks.

WHY IT'S IMPORTANT

Without standard guidance in the form of policies and procedures the organization would quickly devolve into chaos. The likelihood of errors and mistakes would increase considerably if employees were allowed to perform assigned tasks by whatever means they deemed appropriate at the time. Paired with appropriate training, policies and procedures allow for sustainable, repeatable performance that enhances employee safety, protects the equipment, and contributes to the ultimate goals of the business.

Executives have established clear expectations. Leaders are leading by example and coaching on this expectation. None of this matters if the individual worker doesn't participate. It might seem redundant to ask your employees to follow expectations. After all, the Executives have given directives, so you shouldn't need to ask your workers to comply. Ideally, employees would cheerfully follow the guidance from their leadership, but that just isn't the reality we see every day. Employees always have the option to follow expectations or not. Or they could give just enough effort to appear compliant while not fully embracing an expectation. Either way, they are not really following expectations but instead giving half-hearted effort.

The REMEDY Matrix defines the roles and responsibilities of each level of the organization. Employees need to understand that everyone will be held accountable to do their part; themselves included. It's a simple ask but something that is often not directly asked—*Follow Expectations.*

How To Do It

Written guidance to direct employee actions is especially important in the actual performance of the task and the preparation leading up to it.

Employees are expected to perform all tasks in accordance with policies, procedures, and guidelines at all levels of the organization. Whether you are an HR manager hiring employees, an operator starting a pump in the plant, or a warehouse supervisor ordering supplies, you should be following written guidance for that task that will provide the steps to complete the task in a consistent, predictable, and error-free manner.

Sometimes employees fall into the HP trap of overconfidence because they are so familiar with the task. This contributes to them forgetting what is required because they don't follow the expectations. In a study of 86 accidents in biofuel facilities since 2003, researchers found that the primary latent condition contributing to the accidents was operator overconfidence due to the perceived simplicity of the system. They found a scarcity of written procedures and process guidelines to direct operator actions.[27]

According to *The Business Journal*, slightly less than half of employees strongly agree they know what is expected of them at work. For this reason, policies and procedures should be readily accessible to employees to provide written guidance to direct their actions. Many company policies are explained to new employees in the employee handbook, for example, but according to a recent survey conducted by GuideSpark, only 43% of millennials and 30% of non-millennials have read their employee handbook. The Matrix box reminds Engaged Employees to follow expectations to reduce errors. These expectations should be accessible and familiar.

Employee decisions should be made with adequate consideration for the consequences as a means of controlling and mitigating risk.

Rather than following procedural guidance blindly, the employee should use their training and knowledge to ensure the actions are correct.

WHY THE BEHAVIOR OCCURRED—FORGOT

This is a simple memory lapse. I know I should do it, but it just slipped my mind.

EXAMPLES OF PROACTIONS

DEVELOP communications to all employees reinforcing the expectation to use Human Performance techniques to increase hazard awareness and mitigation. Be specific in your guidance so workers understand exactly what good looks like.

CONDUCT paired observations with 20% of your first-line leadership in the field to assess their understanding and use of Human Performance techniques and ability to coach their teams.

OBSERVE the initial actions of 10% of the employees in the field to determine whether they stop to conduct a 2-Minute Drill or utilize other tools to prevent lapses in awareness.

REVIEW two recent events with the team and assess how Human Performance Tools, such as Self-Checking or Questioning Attitude, would have prevented the event in question.

SHARE a recent example of how focusing on a specific 2-Minute Drill card question prevented a potential recent error. Reinforce the value of considering the 2-Minute Drill card questions before starting work.

HOW THE CULTURE SURVEY HELPS YOU MEASURE EFFECTIVENESS

C1a—Employees follow the company rules.

C1b—Employees conduct their activities the same way, whether they are being observed or not.

C1c—Employees perform tasks in a controlled, deliberate manner.

C1d—Employees are trained in the use of error-reduction techniques.

If your employees would agree with these statements related to *Follow Expectations,* you are on the right track.

EMPLOYEES FOLLOW THE COMPANY RULES (C1a)

Engaged employees will follow the rules, and when they see a potential problem, they will communicate the issue and work to correct it. Policies stating the company's expectations should be shared with employees on a periodic basis to get their feedback. Procedures are in place to direct the activities for a particular task and should be followed as written. When errors or improvements are identified, an approved process is followed to revise the procedure to support continuous improvement. This is an important action because...

> *you aren't interested in having employees who will blindly follow the procedure—you want employees who understand the task, can think about what is being directed, and can make suggestions on how to improve performance.*

EMPLOYEES CONDUCT THEIR ACTIVITIES THE SAME WAY, WHETHER THEY ARE BEING OBSERVED OR NOT (C1b)

When management observations are a routine activity, workers are more likely to conduct business as usual because they don't view the leader's presence as a unique situation. When such observations are more infrequent, workers can be distracted (or just stop working altogether) when managers are around. This is unfortunate because leaders leave the work area with a biased view of what is going on because they didn't really see the actual level of performance. A series of tests were conducted to study the *Hawthorne Effect*, which states that people behave differently when they know they are being watched. For example, workers were told they would be observed during their break time and smoking levels dropped considerably. Doctors were told their handwashing techniques would be observed and handwashing compliance rose over 55%. So, if you want employees to do good work whether or not they are being observed, you need to make it common practice that leaders interact with employees and help them solve problems.

EMPLOYEES PERFORM TASKS IN A CONTROLLED, DELIBERATE MANNER (C1c)

Employees who have the necessary training, correct material and equipment, and proper guidance to do a task will perform the work in a controlled, deliberate manner. They won't be hesitant or doubtful as they proceed. They know what to do and it shows. This situation will look quite different for an employee who is in a hurry for whatever reason or is uncertain about the right steps to take. Often employees may display a level of overconfidence in the performance of a task which will lead them to take actions without using human error reduction techniques such as Self-Checking or Questioning Attitude. A demonstration of this would be incorrectly dialing a phone number and having to hang up and try it again. If you knew you only had one chance to get it right in a life-or-death situation, you would dial the number in a controlled, deliberate manner. Any observer would be able to tell the difference.

EMPLOYEES ARE TRAINED IN THE USE OF ERROR-REDUCTION TECHNIQUES (C1d)

Your friend got you to agree to run a marathon with them in six weeks. You feel like you are in rather good shape, but you've never been a runner, so you don't really know what to expect. Do you think training

156

for the marathon over the next six weeks is a good idea? If you say you don't need to train, you'll have a different view of that decision once you are a couple of miles into the marathon. The same principles apply to our workers when you don't provide training in important areas like error reduction. If you haven't trained them on the traps they need to identify and mitigate, and the Human Performance tools to use to avoid errors, you are just hoping for the best. Reducing errors is clearly a priority for any business because the costs of injuries and rework can be immense and take a real toll on profitability. The priority you place on the delivery of training to reduce errors will pay for itself many times over, both in bottom-line financial results and employee safety and engagement.

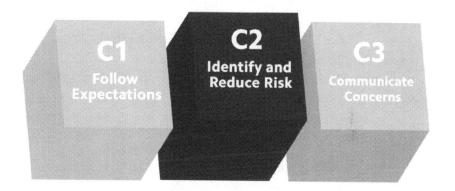

C2: IDENTIFY AND REDUCE RISK

FORMULA: Manage Risk

MATRIX: Engaged Employees

WHY THE BEHAVIOR OCCURRED: Didn't See Risk

Defining "Identify and Reduce Risk"

Employees understand the impact of their actions and value coaching. Make decisions considering unwanted circumstances and actions are taken to mitigate risk.

Why It's Important

It is important to identify all hazards and risks and take the necessary actions to eliminate or mitigate them, but hazard and risk are not synonyms.

A hazard represents a potential source of damage or harm. A risk, on the other hand, depends on our exposure to the hazard. For example, if there is a hole in the ground that is ten feet wide and ten feet deep, that is a hazard. It doesn't become a risk until you have work to do in the vicinity of the hole. Mitigation actions may include establishing a firm barrier around the hole to eliminate the risk (but the hazard is still there!) While the risk is associated with our proximity to the hole, we may want to take mitigating actions anyway just to take the hazard seriously.

Once a hazard is identified, it can be either be eliminated or controlled to reduce the risk. In the example of the hole in the ground, we can eliminate the hazard by filling the hole in with dirt—we've addressed the risk by eliminating the hazard. If that is not practical, then a firm barrier is an effective engineering control that will isolate the people from the hazard (which is still there as we said before), but effectively mitigates the risk. This approach is called the "hierarchy of controls," where elimination of the hazard is the most effective approach.[28]

OSHA states that one of the "root causes" of workplace injuries, illnesses, and incidents is the failure to identify or recognize hazards that are present, or that could have been anticipated.[29] A critical element of any effective safety and health program is a proactive, ongoing process to identify and assess such hazards. The "Examples of Proactions" provided for each block of the Matrix are aligned with this strategy.

How To Do It

By taking a good look around the work area before starting the task, employees can identify existing hazards and associated risks and address them right away. Issues such as housekeeping and tripping hazards should quickly be resolved, but too often the employees just want to get the work done and don't take a few minutes to assess the work area. A key training aid that KnowledgeVine uses is called the Two Minute Drill Card, presented in our online training, that sets employees up for success with how to utilize the card. On one side there are questions that should be asked before the work starts, and on the other side are questions that workers should ask when they get to the work location. Examples of questions on the "Plan the Work" side of the card include "What is my role for this task?" and "Am I qualified and equipped to do this work?" On the "Work the Plan" side of the card, questions include "Are conditions as expected and as briefed?" and "Are hazards and housekeeping issues mitigated?" Asking a few of these fundamental questions is the key to identifying and mitigating risk! Employees often don't realize there was a risk presented by a tripping hazard in the work area until they are on the ground with a twisted ankle—an entirely avoidable situation.

Why The Behavior Occurred—Didn't See Risk

Based on their level of knowledge or level of experience, they don't see something as a hazard or a risk or maybe they lack enough experience to understand something might be dangerous or risky OR their situational awareness was poor, and they completely missed a hazard or risk that they should have mitigated.

EXAMPLES OF PROACTIONS

CONDUCT observations of 10% of the work activities in the field to ensure risk is appropriately considered and mitigated.

ESTABLISH opportunities for workers that do well at identifying and mitigating risk to peer-coach workers who are struggling in this area. Document the coaching and results.

REINFORCE the need for the rules and safety measures by providing a case study, root cause or lessons learned directly related to the issue at hand. (Often workers "won't" because they don't understand "why.")

IDENTIFY the workers struggling with hazard and risk mitigation and target coaching to them. Additionally, provide positive reinforcement to the workers who do it well. Document these efforts.

REVIEW the last three events and determine if any risks were overlooked. Share the results of this review with the entire organization.

HOW THE CULTURE SURVEY HELPS YOU MEASURE EFFECTIVENESS

C2a—Employees are receptive to coaching, and often coach each other.

C2b—Employees are receptive to changes in the organization.

C2c—Employees will not hesitate to stop a coworker if they think their actions are incorrect.

C2d— The actions of employees support the company's success.

If your employees agree with these statements related to *Identify and Reduce Risk,* you are on the right track.

EMPLOYEES ARE RECEPTIVE TO COACHING, AND OFTEN COACH EACH OTHER (C2a)

Most people are good at recognizing hazards, but we could all improve if we're coachable. Being coachable simply means you realize there is a possibility that there's something you haven't learned that could make you better than you are now. It is one of life's most important skills, not just for athletes, but for everyone. You are not coachable if you think you are always right, if you are not open to change, or if you have a negative disposition. Your employees already know which members of the team will be receptive to their coaching, and which are likely to give a sarcastic eyeroll when confronted with a chance to learn something new. Coaching doesn't have to be from the top-down; peer to peer coaching is highly valuable and likely more impactful since a peer has a current understanding of the requirements and can offer valuable feedback if their coworker is willing to receive it. When senior leaders develop a culture of trust in the organization, employees are receptive to coaching and are willing to coach one another because they are confident in their value to the organization and are willing to make improvements to meet the company goals.

EMPLOYEES ARE RECEPTIVE TO CHANGES IN THE ORGANIZATION (C2b)

Employees see vice presidents come and go every few years, and with each new arrival comes a new initiative that promises to deliver big results. But guess what—they rarely do. Part of the problem is the rollout of the new initiative didn't consider the last initiative and the one before that, both of which are still hanging around on life-support. Take a walk down the hall and see what relics you can find of these good ideas from the past. Are there still bulletin boards with announcements or progress reports? Are there procedure references that institutionalize these initiatives? These are the reasons the new idea won't work. Employees are confused by remnants of the past because they don't know if the new thing is replacing the old thing, or will it just be piled on top of it. Besides, this VP will be moving on in a few years, so why get on board? Employees are often not receptive to change in the organization, and for good reason. Leaders must do a better job of communication and planning on the front end if they ever intend to see results down the road.

EMPLOYEES WILL NOT HESITATE TO STOP A COWORKER IF THEY THINK THEIR ACTIONS ARE INCORRECT (C2c)

When an employee feels like they are part of the team and a contributor to the overall success of the company, they come to work with a different attitude than those who do not feel this sense of inclusion. Even if it is an act that is out of their comfort zone, they will likely stop a coworker that is about to make a mistake because they are thinking about the organizational impact, not just the impact on that worker. Some employees will be more receptive to this interjection than others, and in some cases the employee who stops a coworker's actions may ultimately be wrong. The way leaders respond to such a *stop work* event will be significant regarding the culture that is being developed. The response will be even more impactful if the intervention was unnecessary because the action was NOT incorrect. There should be positive recognition for the behavior if it was well-intentioned because the questioning attitude is right, even if it was wrong.

THE ACTIONS OF EMPLOYEES SUPPORT THE COMPANY'S SUCCESS (C2d)

If employees are going to have a positive impact on the organization, they need to know how their actions align with the company goals. If the company goals are well thought out, it should not be difficult to link every task an employee performs to one or more of the goals. If that is hard to do then the task may be unnecessary, or the goals need to be revised. One of the Executive actions in the Matrix requires occasional observation of work activities to ensure alignment with business strategies. This is evidence of the unique role of each level in the organization as the Executives set the goals and strategy, and Employees seek clear alignment in everything they do to support the achievement of these goals. In this way Engaged Employees contribute their experiences, skills, and abilities to help the organization succeed.

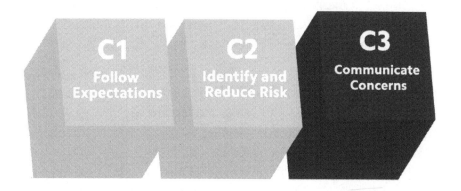

C3: COMMUNICATE CONCERNS

FORMULA: Error Defenses

MATRIX: Engaged Employees

WHY THE BEHAVIOR OCCURRED: Didn't Stop

DEFINING "COMMUNICATE CONCERNS"

Near misses and LOWs are reported to strengthen error defenses. Employees stop and seek guidance from supervision when unsure or out of scope.

WHY IT'S IMPORTANT

A key component of effective error defenses is the timely communication of concerns by employees. Engaged employees are keenly aware of deficiencies and potential problems and are more likely to identify them so they can be corrected. Employees who are not so engaged will likely not be aware of such issues and may be reluctant to report them even when recognized. Part of the problem may be that these employees are confused by the language. For example:

NEAR MISS: OSHA defines a near miss as "an unplanned event that did not result in injury, illness or damage—but had the potential to do so." Some have changed the name to *good catch* and found success in getting employees engaged in identification and communication of these potential issues.

Latent Organizational Weakness (LOW): The term is also unfamiliar to most workers. A LOW is an undetected deficiency in organizational processes and values that create workplace conditions that provoke error or degrade the integrity of defenses. Leaders should be able to explain this concept in simple terms so workers can internalize the meaning. For example, LOWs are conditions that you may not recognize that set you up for potential failure or injury. They are lingering issues just waiting to cause problems because someone else failed to correct them and passed the issue along to you. Examples include incorrect procedures, inaccurate training materials, inconsistent expectations, or process workarounds.

How To Do It

When employees understand the terms, they are more likely to get involved in identification and resolution of these issues. Also, according to the National Safety Council, employees will be reluctant to report deficiencies if they are fearful, may be embarrassed, if it is too difficult to report it, if they sense a loss of reputation, or if they experience peer pressure. Leaders should address each of these issues to increase the likelihood of employee reporting of near misses and LOWs.

Some organizations track *stop work* as a measure of lost productivity. The thinking is if you are stopped, you aren't producing, and you aren't making any money. This approach is contrary to a Human Performance culture. To encourage workers to stop when they are unsure (and likely prevent errors or injuries that could result), consider tracking how often your employees had the courage to stop the work. In this case, you are measuring stop work as a positive behavior that should be encouraged. Of course, you want your workers to understand the consequences of such an action (lost revenue, for example) but you also want to value their decision not to proceed when they were unsure or felt they were off-track. This promotes a culture of continuous improvement and establishes a strong error-defense within the organization.

WHY THE BEHAVIOR OCCURRED—DIDN'T STOP

While engaged in the work, the employee failed to recognize drifting conditions, scope change, or elements of the plan that were no longer working. The employee failed to stop work to communicate and address these changes with leadership, resulting in an error or noncompliance with the rule. An example of this may be a worker who inadvertently entered an area flagged off as a drop zone, or an employee that is unsure about as assigned task but chooses to proceed in the face of uncertainty.

EXAMPLES OF PROACTIONS

INTERVIEW a sample of employees (3-5%) to see how they respond to off-normal conditions or changes in the work plan.

OBSERVE several JSA meetings to evaluate whether off-normal conditions are discussed, and if adequate directions are given to employees when these conditions arise.

REVIEW the stop work policy and evaluate its effectiveness by assessing the incidences of stop work execution over the previous week, month, and year. Report these findings to the team and encourage greater participation in the stop work process If necessary.

PREPARE communications to all employees about scope creep and how this can present unforeseen hazards when they don't stop to address the new conditions.

EVALUATE the near-miss, good catch process to ensure it meets the following minimum criteria: expectations of usage are clear, the reporting option is easy-to-use, non-punitive, and anonymous and provides positive reinforcement for reporting.

HOW THE CULTURE SURVEY HELPS YOU MEASURE EFFECTIVENESS

C3a—Employees think it is important to report all problems or close calls right away.

C3b—Employees believe every task can be done without error or injury.

C3c—When employees are unsure about a task it is OK to stop.

C3D—Employees are comfortable challenging existing conditions.

If your employees would agree with these statements related to *Communicate Concerns,* you are on the right track.

EMPLOYEES THINK IT IS IMPORTANT TO REPORT ALL PROBLEMS OR CLOSE CALLS RIGHT AWAY (C3a)

In many organizations, an employee who cuts their finger at work might put their hand in their pocket and hide the injury rather than tell their boss. Maybe they remember a coworker who reported a minor injury in the past and was sent home without pay, or maybe it reset the safe-days-at-work record and he became a victim of ridicule. Basically, they fear some sort of retaliation if they report the injury even though the management team says they should. Or maybe the forms and reports that are required are so cumbersome the employee thinks twice about reporting the issue for fear of being sucked into an administrative chasm. You want employees to report any problem they see so you can fix it before it becomes a bigger issue. The same is true of close calls, or near-misses, because if someone almost got hurt, you are just lucky they weren't standing in a different position, or you could have a serious injury on your hands. You need to treat such reporting as a gift, one that allows you to correct a deficiency without having to suffer the consequences of a real event.

EMPLOYEES BELIEVE EVERY TASK CAN BE DONE WITHOUT ERROR OR INJURY (C3b)

Humans are fallible and even the best make mistakes. That is why Error Defenses are a key part of the REMEDY formula because you want to minimize the frequency and severity of the mistakes you are bound to make. Employees need to understand the processes and training in place to prevent errors because they should enter every task with the mindset that it can be completed without error or injury. When you think about after-injury investigations, there are always missed opportunities to have prevented the accident. Maybe the wrong tool was used, the procedure was incorrect, or there were distractions not considered. Each of these represents a precursor to the error, that if properly addressed, would have reduced the likelihood of the event. We know that humans make mistakes, which is why we establish error defenses and deliver training to ensure every task can be done without incident.

WHEN EMPLOYEES ARE UNSURE ABOUT A TASK IT IS OK TO STOP (C3c)

Stopping an in-progress activity takes a lot of confidence, and courage. There can be a considerable amount of second-guessing to convince yourself it is probably ok, so often employees talk themselves out of speaking up. "What if I'm wrong and I stop this work and cost the company a lot of money?" "I stopped a job after I'd been here a few months and they told me I didn't know what I was looking at—maybe they were right!" Regardless of the second-guessing, employees need to stop if they are unsure. Granted, it would be better to ensure they get their questions answered and fully understand the expectations before they get started, but that is in the past. They shouldn't try to figure it out as they go because that will lead to trouble. It needs to be ok for employees to stop when they're unsure and the way management reacts to this action will serve to set the culture for everyone. If safety is a top priority, which it is, then employees need to stop before they take another step.

EMPLOYEES ARE COMFORTABLE CHALLENGING EXISTING CONDITIONS (C3d)

Employees need to feel the freedom to voice their opinion, but in many cases they don't. They fear isolation or punitive actions if they speak up and are often branded as troublemakers if they do. If you want employees to feel engaged, you need to ensure they are free to *communicate concerns* and make suggestions to change existing processes. Every employee challenge will not be met with a swift action plan, nor should it be, but hearing employee concerns, and making sure they are comfortable sharing them, is an essential part of developing an effective organization. Often the employee does not have the big-picture view that management does. Sometimes they just don't know, but that doesn't mean they should be silenced. Encourage employees to voice their opinion and challenge the status quo. A famous quote from Henry Ford was, "They can have their car in any color, as long as it is black." Wouldn't it be interesting to have a video of the first employee that suggested they offer to paint the cars in different colors!

PART III
Now That You Know

"If you can't explain it simply, you don't understand it well enough."

~ Albert Einstein (1879 – 1955)

This book started with the question, "When you first learned Human Performance, was it easy or difficult?"

When tackling a challenge like creating a Human Performance culture, you knew it would not be an easy task; otherwise, you would have done it long ago. However, being difficult is no excuse to continue with a current cycle that doesn't work. There are no shortcuts to excellence, but since you are still reading, you know this—and are likely willing to put in the work. Hopefully, this book has revealed a path that is efficient, effective, most likely to yield long-term results, and a good use of your efforts.

However, we are talking about culture change. As you recall from the Culture Cycle discussion, there needs to be continuous influence on your team's belief, behaviors, results, and experiences until any change becomes *habit strength* and is permanent. This is not a one-person challenge. It will take effort from many people in your organization. Your job now is to *sell* these concepts to the rest of your organization to gain support and get some help. After all, as we've read many times, "many hands make light work."

It would be great to hand a copy of *REMEDY* to every member of your organization, but the reality is you might have a difficult time motivating people to read it. You can't walk into the breakroom and say, "Do you have an hour? I want to show you a great process to improve our organization. As you can see from my 30-slide PowerPoint we will cover culture change, how our current culture is fighting change, why we need Human Performance, how the Culture Cycle can help us understand influencing culture, REMEDY Human Performance, the REMEDY formula, the REMEDY Matrix, how to identify risk, understand why we have risk, the roadmap for Human Performance culture change (DIAS), proactions we take to target organizational deficiencies..."

The first question might be, "Where did you get that projector and screen?" Followed closely by, "Do you think I have nothing else to do?"

If you're going to get buy-in so you have *many hands* within your organization working on implementing Human Performance, you're going to need to explain it simply.

Don't overwhelm your colleagues. Don't tell them how an internal combustion engine works; tell them how awesome it is to drive a car.

This final chapter provides you with an empowering tool—an outline to help communicate the forest without getting others lost in the trees. As we present this, you will find you probably have a much deeper understanding than is necessary to explain it. This is good. If you are able to pique someone's interest, they may have questions and now you have the answers. But to start the conversation, and to paraphrase Einstein, "you should explain it simply." If they want to go deeper, great, but for now, just describe the forest.

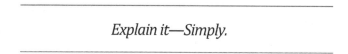

Explain it—Simply.

WHY IS THERE RISK?

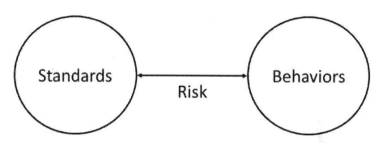

Risk is found in the gap between the standards (work as directed) and the behaviors (work as performed). If the standards are wrong, it creates risk from which employees must work around to get work done. If the standards are right, but workers aren't following them, then the worker is creating risk. To eliminate this risk, you need good standards and behaviors that meet expectations. Risk is found in the gap between standards and behaviors.

HOW DO YOU FIND RISK?

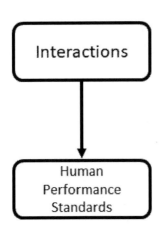

The simplest way to identify risk is to assess workplace behaviors against an established standard. To ensure the entire staff is on the same page and coaching achieves a high standard, you would do well to implement a fully detailed Human Performance process. Otherwise, you are just sending leaders into the field to coach on whatever catches their eye that day. If you establish Human Performance as the standard, then workers know what is expected and how to demonstrate it, and leaders have a clear standard to coach. When you know the standard is right, you can easily identify the risk created by misaligned behaviors while people are engaged in work. In-field coaching should be done through the lens of Human Performance. If the behaviors seen are aligned with Human Performance standards, then you should give positive reinforcement to workers to prevent drifting back into risky behaviors. If the behaviors are misaligned, then you know there is risk, and you need to coach people to align with the standards to eliminate this risk.

HOW DO YOU ELIMINATE IT?

Two ways: in-the-moment coaching and broader coaching on negative trends.

During interactions, coaches use Human Performance as the standard to assess jobsite behaviors. If something is missed, real-time coaching is given to move behaviors closer to the standards, immediately closing the risk gap.

You also need to start going a level deeper in coaching to understand WHY the risky behavior occurred. Capturing and trending this WHY data allows you to identify and coach on broader behavior trends. This helps to close the risk gap for others that may not have been directly observed but are struggling with the same issues. Once you understand WHY you can trend the cause and address the issue more accurately.

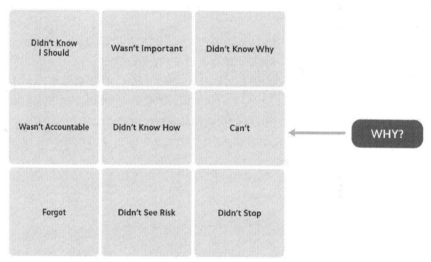

HOW DO YOU KNOW IF THE ISSUE IS A WORKER BEHAVIOR OR AN ORGANIZATIONAL WEAKNESS?

Once you know WHY you can start to close in on the real issue. For example, if people didn't know there was a standard, then the organization may have done a poor job of communicating it. In this case, the organization needs to do a better job of setting expectations. If workers don't know how, there needs to be better training and coaching. If it's discovered that workers know what to do, and how to do it, but are frequently forgetting, then organizations need to reinforce Human Performance techniques, like Self-Checking or Peer-Checking, to increase situational awareness.

Notice the top two rows are organizational weaknesses—things organizations should be doing better. If people don't know WHY they should be doing something or CAN'T do something because they aren't equipped, then it's not a worker problem; it's an organizational problem. Now you can work on fixing the issue for everyone, creating better workplace standards, and eliminating this risk for everyone, not just the people who were seen struggling with it.

If the trend is in the bottom row, then you need to work on individual behaviors. Help them to remember with Human Performance methodologies. Look at remediation or discipline for the person that knows what to do and is equipped to do it but willfully and intentionally chooses to not comply. Reinforce *stop-work authority* and *near-miss reporting* so teams know, without a doubt, that *stopping when unsure* is the expectation.

Trends

How Do You Target Corrective Action?

Now that you know WHAT kind of problem you have, you can specifically target the right response.

If the issue is found to be an organizational weakness, then you know you need to take action to fix the system and improve the standards. If the standards are correct and easy to comply with, then less opportunities are created for workers to deviate from the standards, and you have less risk.

If the trend indicates individual issues, then you know you need to coach the employees to get their behaviors closer to the standards. If you can help the workers to meet the standards, you can close the risk gap.

The Complete REMEDY Cycle For Organizational Improvement And Culture Change

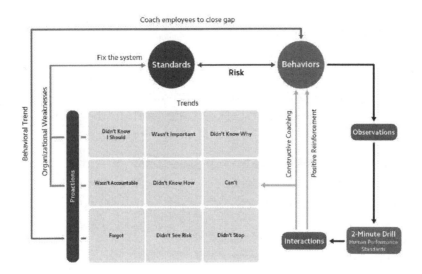

Remember, this is a high-level discussion about a complex issue, implementing and sustaining Human Performance. This should be sufficient to give anyone a view of the forest without dragging them through the trees. They need to understand the strategy and start wrapping their heads around the tactics of a robust Human Performance process. Don't overwhelm them with too much information too soon. The goal is to start creating curiosity, which grows into knowledge seeking, that creates allies, and builds a guiding coalition within your organization to create a Human Performance culture.

As discussed earlier, to influence the Culture Cycle, you need to continually influence the beliefs, behaviors, results, and experiences of your team; that's your strategy. Looking at the process above you can start to see some of the tactics.

- You can influence beliefs by providing effective training, setting clear expectations, improving your standards/work processes, or coaching on behavior trends.

- You can influence the behaviors through in-field interactions that provide real-time coaching.

- Positive results, which are consistent, repeatable, and don't rely on luck, should start to become the norm.

The experience should change dramatically for your workers. Suddenly supervisors are seeking to understand WHY a behavior occurred instead of just pointing out compliance issues. Leadership is taking targeted actions to get to the root cause of problems and not just mass-emailing *awareness* messages. The system is being fixed so the worker doesn't feel like it's Groundhog Day as they deal with the same problems over and over.

This shift in experience is now shaping their beliefs in what *good looks like* and how doing their part can help the overall effort. And the cycle continues, only now their belief in Human Performance is strengthened because they have the experience to back up their initial training. Your constant engagement influences the workers' belief that they can *wait it out* and hope this new expectation goes away. You start to develop a "I don't know how they did it at your last job, but here..." mentality that impacts the beliefs of new hires or even people who are slow to get off the sidelines. The barge is off the bank and in the safe waters of the river channel. The heavy lifting is done, but you know you need to keep your hands on the wheel to avoid drifting back into the old culture.

This is KnowledgeVine's process, created from decades of experience and some hard learned lessons. While we believe it is the most robust, comprehensive, user-friendly, and sustainable process available, it's not the only Human Performance process out there. The hope is that you have gained the knowledge you need to guide you through your next steps of performance improvement. Use what you now know to:

START the conversations within your organization.

KICKSTART your current HP program that may have plateaued.

CREATE your own process for implementing HP in your organization.

RECOGNIZE the pitfalls to avoid or strategies to consider when moving along the HP path.

ASSESS the offerings of consultants or trainers that you are considering.

COMPLETE a postmortem on a previous attempt at culture change that may have failed.

CONVINCE the person in your organization holding the checkbook that you have a well-thought out, high-probability-of-success plan they need to fund.

BUILD a coalition within your organization ready to support change and finally get that ball rolling.

Creating a Human Performance culture is a challenging but worthwhile endeavor. Many people get overwhelmed with the perceived enormity of shaping their organization. You, however, now have the knowledge and tools to recognize and mitigate the potential traps of culture change. You are equipped to effectively navigate your organization to safer, more reliable, efficient, and productive performance. You also now have the *curse of knowledge*. Now that you know, you're obligated to act. If it still feels overwhelming, there are communities of Human Performance practitioners you can join to get support. There are other books, webinars, and conferences where you can gain more information and insight. You can also reach out to KnowledgeVine directly (www.knowledgevine.com) to help you or your contractors to start adopting a Human Performance culture. The next move is yours and it's not hyperbole to say that lives may be hanging in the balance.

Back to the query, "When you first learned Human Performance, was it easy or difficult?" Now you can confidently answer this question with, "It's complex, but worth the effort, and I have the REMEDY to make an evolving Human Performance culture possible."

GLOSSARY

BEHAVIORS: Employee actions that are observable in the work area (work as performed)

CULTURE CYCLE: Beliefs influence behaviors. Behaviors create results. Results inform experiences. Experiences shape beliefs. Beliefs influence behaviors...you can influence the Culture Cycle in many ways, at any stage, to get the behaviors and results you desire.

DISTRACTIONS: One of the Core Four Human Performance Traps that can be found in areas where there are high noise levels, constant interruptions by phones or coworkers, and in places where more than one task is being conducted simultaneously.

DRIFT: The tendency for behaviors to move away from the required standard, either due to lack of enforcement or confusion over what the standard requires. Also referred to as Normalization of Deviation.

EFFECTIVE COMMUNICATION: One of the Core Four Human Performance Tools that ensures you are speaking and listening in a way that eliminates the potential for mistakes. Using three-part communication, the phonetic alphabet, and individually pronouncing numerals are all ways to effectively communicate.

EMPOWERED LEADERS: Employees below the Director level have direct reports. As defined in the REMEDY Matrix, they are "A strengthened leadership team committed to continuous improvement and entrusted with the authority to take action."

ENGAGED EMPLOYEES: Employees with no direct reports. As defined in the REMEDY Matrix, Engaged Employees are "A knowledgeable workforce that contributes to the organization's success by making conservative decisions and sharing the challenges of their work."

HUMAN PERFORMANCE: A continuous improvement process for creating an organizational culture that is focused on reducing the frequency and severity of human error by improving both individual behaviors and workplace standards.

INFORMED EXECUTIVES: Employees at the Director level and above, typically those with decision-making authority, which have Leaders reporting to them. As defined in the REMEDY Matrix, Informed Executives establish "A learning organization, with a culture of trust, where information flows between all levels."

JSA: A Job Safety Analysis is a safety tool that can be used to define and control hazards associated with a certain process, job, or procedure. Also called JHA (job hazard analysis), JSB (job safety briefing), etc.

LOW: Acronym for Latent Organizational Weakness

LATENT ORGANIZATIONAL WEAKNESS: Undetected deficiencies in processes, equipment or values that create job-site conditions that either provoke error or degrade the integrity of controls. It is simpler to describe LOWs as *snakes in the grass* that are lying in wait for an unsuspecting passer-by.

ORGANIZATIONAL CULTURE: The sum of the individual behaviors an organization's people exhibit day after day.

OVERCONFIDENCE: One of the Core Four Human Performance Traps that causes people to overestimate their knowledge, underestimate risks, and exaggerate their ability to control events.

PEER-CHECK: One of the Core Four Human Performance Tools, performed by two workers who are side-by-side before and during the action. Before the performer takes the action, the Peer-Checker verbally confirms the action is correct.

PRINCIPLES OF HUMAN PERFORMANCE:

Principle #1: Humans will always make mistakes

Principle #2: Implement strategies to predict, prevent, and manage error-likely situations

Principle #3: Identify and correct organizational weaknesses

Principle #4: Use positive reinforcement to achieve higher levels of performance

Principle #5: Review and learn from past experience to improve future performance

PROACTIONS: Proactive, predefined actions taken to address an identified gap or deficiency in organizational performance.

QUESTIONING ATTITUDE: One of the Core Four Human Performance Tools that asks, "What is the worst thing that is most likely to happen to me, my peer, or my team?" Questioning Attitude is a Tool used by individuals and teams. As an individual, a worker considers the consequences of their actions if performed incorrectly as opposed to the likelihood of it going wrong. In a team setting, the same worker asks their teammates questions to ensure there are no misunderstandings.

REMEDY FORMULA: RE+M+ED → Y where the following stand for:

RE	Reduce Errors
M	Manage Risk
ED	Errors Defenses
Y	Yield or Return on Investment

REMEDY MATRIX: A graphical representation of the organization having a shared strategy that defines the different roles and responsibilities when it comes to creating a Human Performance culture.

RISK: The gap between the Standards (work as directed) and the Behaviors (work as performed)

SELF-CHECK: One of the Core Four Human Performance Tools to help an individual focus on the task they are about to perform (STAR—Stop, Think, Act and Review).

STANDARDS: Expectations that establish what workers are required to do (work as directed).

STRETCH GOALS: Those goals, which are identified as high effort and high risk, and intentionally set above normal standards to attract rewards, opportunities, and experience. Not expected to be fully achieved, they are often set to inspire growth and counter team complacency.

TIME PRESSURE: One of the Core Four Human Performance Traps that can appear on the job in many forms; due dates, daily schedules, and customer requests are just a few. Time Pressure is often self-imposed. Since you cannot remove all the Time Pressure, the key to success is in recognizing the Trap and making conscious decisions about how to deal with it.

VAGUE GUIDANCE: One of the Core Four Human Performance Traps that becomes evident when directions lack the necessary detail, leaving room to "fill in the blanks." This trap applies to both verbal instruction and written documents.

REFERENCES

1. https://www.commerce.senate.gov/index.php/services/files/21A88848-6085-4C26-A5AF-41643BD2BDB9

2. Grinstein, J. (2020, February 27). *What the Challenger Disaster Teaches Us About Speaking Up In A New Era of Spaceflight.* Your Brain at Work.

3. Berger, B. (2013, January 29). *Columbia Reports Faults in NASA Culture Government Oversight.* Space.

4. Britannica PROCON. (2012, April 26). *Is Nuclear Power Safe for Humans and the Environment?* https://alternativeenergy.procon.org/questions/is-nuclear-power-safe-for-humans-and-the-environment/

5. Office of Nuclear Energy. (2021, March 24). *Nuclear Power is the Most Reliable Energy Source and It's Not Even Close.* Energy.gov.

6. Lipman, V. (2023, September 4). *New Study Explores Why Change Management Fails – And How To (Perhaps) Succeed.* Forbes.

7. Bodell, L. (2022, March 28). *"Most Change Initiatives Fail—Here's How to Beat the Odds."* Forbes.

8. LaGrone, Sam. (2019, August 6). *NTSB: Lack of Navy Oversight, Training Were Primary Cause of Fatal McCain Collision.* USNI News. https://news.usni.org/2019/08/06/ntsb-lack-of-navy-oversight-training-were-primary-causes-of-fatal-mccain-collision

9. https://usma.org/wp-content/uploads/2015/06/1136a.pdf

10. Gallup Inc (2022). State of the Global Marketplace. New York: GALLUP PRESS

11. Gallup Inc. (2017). State of the Global Workplace. New York: GALLUP PRESS.

12. Gallup Inc. (2017) *State of the American Worlqplacc.* New York. GALLUP PRESS.

13. Kaplan R. & Norton, D. (2001). *The Strategy-Focused Organization,* Harvard Business School Press

14. Gallup Inc. (2017*) State of the American Workplace*. New York: GALLUP PRESS.

15. Gallup Inc. (2023) State of the American Workplace. New York: GALLUP PRESS.

16. The Niagara Institute (2022) "Leadership Survey Results: 13 Statistics from Leaders Worldwide."

17. Lipman, V. (2016, February 4). *The Best Managers Always Lead by Example*. Forbes. https://www.forbes.com/sites/victorlipman/2016/02/04/the-best-managers-always-lead-by-example/?sh=33447f1c279d

18. Kiisel, Ty. (2012, October 16). *65% of Americans Choose Better Boss Over a Raise— Here's Why*. Forbes. https://www.forbes.com/sites/tykiisel/2012/10/16/65-of-americans-choose-a-better-boss-over-a-raise-heres-why/?sh=1e07a22f76d2

19. Apollo Technical (2023, June 22). 17 Employee Recognition Statistics That Will Make You Think.

20. Miller, J. (2017, September 19). *More Than Half of New Managers Fail. Here's How to Avoid Their Common Mistakes*. Inc.com. https://www.inc.com/jeff-miller/more-than-half-of-new-managers-fail-heres-how-to-a.html

21. Charan, R. (2011). *The Leadership Pipeline: How to Build the Leadership Powered Company*. Jossey-Bass.

22. Charan, R. (2011). *The Leadership Pipeline: How to Build the Leadership Powered Company*. Jossey-Bass.

23. Morris, S. (2015, June 25). *4 Strategies for Clearly Communicating Expectations*. The Complete Leader. https://www.thecompleteleader.org/articles/4-strategies-clearly-communicating-expectations

24. Finklestein S. R. & Fishbach, A. (2012). *Tell me what I did wrong: Experts seek and respond to negative feedback*. Journal of Consumer Research, 39(1), 22–38. https://doi.org/10.1086/661934

25. Kanter, Rosabeth M. (2015) *MOVE: Putting America's Infrastructure Back in the Lead*. New York: W. W. Norton & Company.

26. Lowe, C.M. (2006, December 15). *Accidents waiting to happen: the contribution of latent conditions to patient safety*. NIH, National Library of Medicine. https://www.ncbi.nlm.nih.gov/pmc/articles/PMC2464871/

27. Calvo Olivares, Romina & Rivera, Selva & Núñez McLeod, Jorge. (2014). *Analysis of Active Failures and Latent Conditions on Biodiesel Production Facilities*. Lecture Notes in Engineering and Computer Science. II. 1013-1017.

28. https://www.osha.gov/sites/default/files/Hierarchy_of_Controls_02.01.23_form_508_2.pdf

29. OSHA.gov/safety-management/hazard-identification

CULTURE SURVEY INDEX

A3: STRENGTHEN DEFENSES

Executives anticipate problems and take actions to prevent them. (page 121)

The company has a formal process in place to correct identified problems. (page121)

Employee development and training are important to the company. (page 122)

Executives are always looking for ways to improve the company. (page 123)

B1: LEAD BY EXAMPLE

Leaders never encourage anyone to bypass the rules. (page 129)

Leaders model the right behaviors and lead by example. (page 129)

Leaders act in a way that reflects the company's values. (page 130)

Leaders clearly communicate their expectations. (page 130)

B2: PROVIDE COACHING

Leaders seek to understand the employee's point of view. (page 141)

Leaders hold employees accountable to standards and expectations. (page 142)

Leaders actively develop employees by providing specific, constructive feedback. (page 142)

Leaders provide positive reinforcement of proper behaviors. (page 143)

B3: Identify and Correct LOWs

Leaders quickly resolve issues. (page 148)

Leaders have the authority to correct issues that impact job performance. (page 149)

Leaders encourage employees to identify and report work-related issues. (page 149)

When an event occurs, we take the right actions to make sure it doesn't happen again. (page 150)

C1: Follow Expectations

Employees follow the company rules. (page 157)

Employees conduct their activities the same way, whether they are being observed or not. (page 157)

Employees perform tasks in a controlled, deliberate manner. (page 158)

Employees are trained in the use of error-reduction techniques. (page 158)

C2: Identify and Reduce Risk

Employees are receptive to coaching, and often coach each other. (page 163)

Employees are receptive to changes in the organization. (page 163)

Employees will not hesitate to stop a coworker if they think their actions are incorrect. (page 164)

The actions of employees support the company's success. (page 164)

C3: COMMUNICATE CONCERNS

Employees think it is important to report all problems or close calls right away. (page 168)

Employees believe every task can be done without error or injury. (page 169)

When employees are unsure about a task it is OK to stop. (page 169)

Employees are comfortable challenging existing conditions. (page 170)

ABOUT THE AUTHORS

DAVID BOWMAN

David W. Bowman is well known as a true Human Performance practitioner with a thorough and strong working knowledge of the topic.

His 30-plus year background in both the utility and petroleum refining industries lends support to the science, application, and data collection necessary to establish and maintain a true culture of performance improvement.

With military experience from the United States Marine Corps, a strong operational background with Chevron, and multiple diverse leadership roles within Entergy, David has the innate ability to assist any organization with establishing an exceptionally reliable culture.

TODD BRUMFIELD

Todd Brumfield brings over 30 years of operations experience to KnowledgeVine. He's served in Director-level positions at several utilities in the United States with responsibility for areas including training, oversight, corrective action and self-assessment, nuclear security, regulatory assurance, and emergency preparedness. He also served as the Director of Performance Improvement in Abu Dhabi, UAE, establishing the initial programs for corrective action, quality assurance and management observation.

As a Team Leader at the World Association of Nuclear Operators, Todd led diverse, multi-disciplined teams in evaluation of plant performance at facilities all over the world. As an inaugural member of the WANO Hong Kong office, he led the development of the Pre-Startup Performance Objectives and Criteria which serves as the guidance document for evaluation of all new nuclear facilities.

He earned a Bachelor's in Nuclear Engineering Technology from Edison State, and an MBA from Nova Southeastern University. Additionally, he earned a Senior Reactor Operator license from NRC and is a certified Six Sigma Black Belt.

KEN HALLARAN

Ken Hallaran has over 20 years of utility and nuclear power industry experience.

He started his career in the United States Navy Nuclear Power Program. After six years he moved into the commercial nuclear industry where he held the roles of Operator, Lab Technician, Specialist, Supervisor and Department Manager. Ken also obtained a Bachelor's degree in Nuclear Engineering Technology.

Throughout his career, Ken has become well versed in Human Performance, organizational improvement, leadership, and causal analysis. His experience as a field worker, supervisor, and manager has given him the ability to be effective in multiple areas and levels of an organization.

Dr. JAMES MERLO

Prior to joining KnowledgeVine, James Merlo was at the North American Electric Reliability Corporation (NERC) as a Vice President and Director of the Reliability Risk Management department. In this role, he led the electric reliability organization's efforts to assess the industry vulnerabilities with regard to events on the Bulk Electric System and how Human Performance challenges affected system reliability.

James served over 22 years in a variety of leadership roles in the US Army, including combat tours in Desert Storm and Operation Iraqi Freedom. Significant positions include Deputy Brigade Commander in Baghdad, Iraq 2004-2005, and as an assistant professor and program director at the United States Military Academy.

Dr. Merlo earned his Bachelor of Science in Human Factors Psychology from West Point, his Masters in Engineering Psychology from the University of Illinois, and his PhD in Applied Experimental and Human Factors Psychology from the University of Central Florida. He is the author of over 50 publications on the subjects of Human Factors Engineering and Human Performance.

DAVE SOWERS

Dave Sowers has over 30 years of experience in power generation and the utility industry.

He started his career in the US Naval Nuclear Power Program where he served aboard the aircraft carrier USS George Washington (CVN-73). After the Navy, Dave started working in commercial nuclear power as an operator and trainer in New Jersey and Louisiana. Dave returned to government service with US Army Corps of Engineers at a hydro-electric dam in Alabama. Throughout his career, Dave has served in many diverse roles including Plant Operator and Trainer, Emergency Responder, Control Room Supervisor, Power Plant Manager, Vice President, and Chief Financial Officer.

In addition to the technical training received in the US Navy, Dave has a Bachelor of Science degree in Resources Management from Troy University, a Master of Science in Management degree from Troy University, and a Master of Science in Emergency Management and Homeland Security from George Washington University.

ABOUT KNOWLEDGEVINE

KnowledgeVine is committed to reducing the frequency and severity of workplace errors by helping organizations leverage and implement Human Performance Improvement training.

Founded in 2014, and recapitalized by Alliant Insurance Services in 2023, KnowledgeVine has taught Human Performance and leadership methodologies to industries across the United States, including utility generation facilities, electrical distribution and transmission, warehouses, oil and gas pipelines, and vegetation companies to name a few.

KnowledgeVine has trained tens of thousands of individuals engaged in Human Performance culture. Continually adapting their training to fit the needs of the user, KnowledgeVine uses technology, in-person training, in-field observations, and coaching to help their clients achieve a safe, efficient, and evolving work environment. If you are interested in learning more about their training and services, please visit www.knowledgevine.com.

KnowledgeVine is frequently requested to speak at various forums; if you are interested in having KnowledgeVine present at your conference or meeting, please visit their website at www.knowledgevine.com.

NOTES...

REMEDY®

REMEDY®

REMEDY®

REMEDY®

REMEDY®

REMEDY®